Better Homes & Gardens

wonder pot

HOUGHTON MIFFLIN HARCOURT
BOSTON · NEW YORK · 2018

BETTER HOMES AND GARDENS® WONDER POT

Editor: Jessica Christensen

Contributing Editors: Annie Krumhardt, Mary Williams

Contributing Copy Editor and Proofreader: Carrie Truesdell, Gretchen Kauffman

Test Kitchen Director: Lynn Blanchard

Test Kitchen Product Supervisor: Colleen Weeden

Test Kitchen Culinary Professionals: Sarah Brekke, Linda Brewer, Carla Christian, Juli Hale, Sammy Mila

Contributing Photographers: Jason Donnelly, Blaine Moats, Jacob Fox, Carson Downing, Andy Lyons

Contributing Food Stylists: Greg Luna, Kelsey Bulat, Dianna Nolin, Charlie Worthington

Administrative Assistant: Marlene Todd

BETTER HOMES AND GARDENS®

Editor in Chief: Stephen Orr

Creative Director: Jennifer D. Madara

Executive Food Editor: Jan Miller

Design Director: Stephanie Hunter

HOUGHTON MIFFLIN HARCOURT

Executive Editor, Brands: Anne Ficklen

Managing Editor: Marina Padakis Lowry

Art Director: Tai Blanche

Production Director: Tom Hyland

WATERBURY PUBLICATIONS, INC.

Design Director: Ken Carlson

Associate Design Director: Doug Samuelson

Production Assistant: Mindy Samuelson

Our seal assures you that every recipe in *Better Homes and Gardens® Wonder Pot* has been tested in the Better Homes and Gardens® Test Kitchen. This means that each recipe is practical and reliable and meets our high standards of taste appeal. We guarantee your satisfaction with this book for as long as you own it.

Pictured on front cover:
New World Chili, page 214

Take a look!

Each recipe in this book has icons at the top of the page indicating special features about it that you may want to consider when planning dinner. Here's what each means.

POT   SKILLET   SLOW COOKER   PRESSURE COOKER

DUMP AND GO: When time (or energy) is short, look for these words. They mean all you have to do is dump the ingredients in the cooking vessel, crank up the heat, and let it do its thing. So easy!

MAKE AHEAD: If you see these words on the recipe, look for the bonus make-ahead direction to prep your meal ahead of time and cut down on last-minute fuss. Now that's smart!

FAST PREP: These words indicate that a recipe requires 30 minutes or less of actual hands-on time. Then just sit back while your meal cooks to perfection.

CALORIE SMART: Eating healthy these days? Look for this icon! Here are the per-serving criteria for our assessment.
• **MAIN-DISH RECIPES:** No more than 375 calories, 3 grams saturated fat, and 20 grams carbohydrate.
• **ONE-DISH RECIPES:** No more than 575 calories, 5 grams saturated fat, and 20 grams carbohydrate.
• **SIDES:** No more than 200 calories, 2 grams saturated fat, and 20 grams carbohydrate.

*CHECK IT OUT! We love wonder pot recipes, but sometimes it's fun to think outside your everyday pots. Look for fix-and-forget slow cooker recipes throughout this book, then check out two bonus chapters full of our best skillet and pressure cooker recipes.

pick a pot

Pots come in all shapes and sizes—and for good reason. Size, surface area, and depth vary greatly among pots, so the cooking vessel you use can dramatically affect how a recipe works. Read on for a complete rundown of the tools that make one-pot cooking easy and delicious—from side-dish-ready saucepans to feed-a-crowd Dutch ovens. Below are the three basic types of pots you'll find on the market.

DUTCH OVEN: With this stovetop-to-oven pot, you can brown foods and bake them in the same vessel. Made of heavy metal, such as cast iron, some are coated with enamel to prevent the metal from reacting with acidic foods. Products that can go in the oven are labeled "oven-safe" on the packaging or on the bottom of the pot. Many have a maximum oven temperature they can withstand.

SAUCEPAN: Saucepans have tall, straight sides with a tight-fitting lid and a long handle. In general, they range in size from 1 quart to 4 quarts. Some saucepans are oven-safe up to a certain temperature.

COOKING POT OR STOCKPOT: This large, straight-sided pot with two small handles is best used on the stovetop because of its size.

choose the best size for the job

2-QUART: This pot is perfect for quick-cooking side dishes, such as rice and vegetables, and for sweet and savory sauces. Get this pot out for the 2 Ways with Grains recipes *(pages 260–263)*.

3-QUART: This medium-size pot is a great choice for small-batch soups, stews, and chilies. If oven-safe, this pot works well for pot pies and small roasts. Use it to make Pork and Wild Rice Soup *(page 152)* and Stovetop Ravioli Lasagna *(page 102)*.

4- TO 5-QUART: Prepare soups and stews, simmer large-batch sauces, and braise large roasts in this versatile-size pot. It's a great fit for Lentil-Chard Soup *(page 153)* and Sunday Dinner Stew *(page 174)*.

STOCKPOT: Use this large, tall pot for making stock and broth and for boiling pasta. It's also a great option when you're doubling recipes for chili and soup, such as Beefy Texas Chili *(page 194)*, Lasagna Soup *(page 144)*, and Turkey Noodle Soup *(page 148)*.

material matters

What a pan is made of can have a huge impact on how it cooks. Here's what you need to know.

TEFLON NONSTICK: These nonstick pots and pans have a coating infused or bonded to the surface that prevents food from sticking and requires minimal cleanup. Use nonmetal utensils to avoid scratching the coating.

CERAMIC NONSTICK (PFOA-FREE): This type of pot is made of aluminum and coated with a nonstick ceramic surface that does not contain perfluorooctanoic acid (PFOA), which may cause health problems. It conducts heat well, and the nonreactive surface is easy to clean. You can lightly spray with nonstick cooking spray or brush with oil to further increase the nonstick capability.

HARD-ANODIZED ALUMINUM: This type of aluminum pot has been processed so the surface of the pan is nonreactive to acidic ingredients. The heavier the pot, the more evenly it will cook.

STAINLESS STEEL: This sturdy material doesn't scratch or dent easily, and it's nonreactive and easy to clean. However, stainless steel has poor heat conductivity compared with other materials. For better heating, choose one with a core of aluminum or copper, called tri-ply.

CAST IRON: These heavy, sturdy pots absorb, conduct, and retain heat well. Cast iron requires seasoning before use, which creates a natural nonstick finish that prevents the iron from reacting with food. Avoid using soap to clean this pan; just a rinse and a wipe down are all it needs.

CERAMIC-COATED CAST IRON: Enameled cast iron has a hard, shiny layer of glaze that protects the pot from rust and prevents it from reacting with food. Avoid using this pot over very high heat; extreme overheating can cause the surface to crack.

COPPER: The most expensive pots on the market, these heavy, sturdy pans are perhaps the best metal for conducting heat. Copper pots are usually lined with stainless steel to prevent food interactions.

Wine-Braised Short Ribs, *page 18*

slow roasting & braising

Nothing brings out amazing flavor from meat as deliciously as long, slow braising in the oven. Choose from pot roasts, pulled meat sandwiches, even tacos!

FAST PREP

coffee-braised pot roast

PREP: 30 minutes | **ROAST:** 2 hours 30 minutes at 325°F | **MAKES:** 8 servings (4 oz. meat + ¼ cup sauce each)

1 3- to 3½-lb. beef chuck pot roast, trimmed of fat

1 tsp. salt

½ tsp. black pepper

1 Tbsp. vegetable oil

1 large onion, halved and sliced

1 medium green sweet pepper, cut into 2-inch pieces

3 cloves garlic, minced

¾ cup beef broth

1 8-oz. can crushed pineapple (juice pack), undrained

1 Tbsp. instant espresso or French roast coffee powder

¼ tsp. crushed red pepper

¼ tsp. ground allspice

2 lb. sweet potatoes, peeled and cut into 2-inch chunks

1. Preheat oven to 325°F. Sprinkle meat with salt and black pepper. In an oven-safe 6-qt. pot heat oil over medium-high heat. Add meat; cook until browned on all sides. Remove meat from pot and set aside.

2. Add onion, sweet pepper, and garlic to drippings in pot. Cook and stir 4 to 5 minutes or until tender and starting to brown. Return meat to pot. Add the next five ingredients (through allspice). Bring to boiling.

3. Roast, covered, 1¾ hours. Add sweet potatoes to pot. Roast, covered, 45 minutes more or until meat and vegetables are tender. Transfer meat and vegetables to a platter; cover to keep warm.

4. For sauce, bring the cooking liquid in pot to boiling; reduce heat. Simmer, uncovered, 10 to 15 minutes or until slightly thickened. Serve meat and vegetables with sauce. If desired, sprinkle with additional crushed red pepper.

PER SERVING: *345 cal., 9 g fat (3 g sat. fat), 111 mg chol., 539 mg sodium, 24 g carb., 3 g fiber, 9 g sugars, 40 g pro.*

FAST PREP

garlic-bacon pot roast

PREP: 30 minutes | **ROAST:** 2 hours 30 minutes at 325°F
MAKES: 8 servings (4 oz. meat + ⅔ cup vegetables each)

1	3- to 3½-lb. beef chuck pot roast, trimmed of fat
½	tsp. kosher salt
¼	tsp. freshly cracked black pepper
2	Tbsp. olive oil
6	slices applewood-smoked bacon, diced
1½	cups coarsely chopped onion
8	cloves garlic, smashed
1	14.5-oz. can reduced-sodium beef broth
2	Tbsp. snipped fresh thyme
1	Tbsp. snipped fresh rosemary
10	small red and/or yellow new potatoes, quartered
3	medium carrots, cut into 2-inch pieces

1. Preheat oven to 325°F. Sprinkle meat with salt and pepper. In an oven-safe 6-qt. pot heat oil over medium-high heat. Add meat and cook until browned on all sides. Remove meat from pot and set aside.

2. Add bacon to drippings in pot. Cook until browned, stirring occasionally. Drain bacon on paper towels; cover and chill half of the bacon until serving. Add onion and garlic to drippings in pot. Cook and stir about 5 minutes or until onion is tender and starting to brown. Return roast and remaining bacon to pot. Add broth, thyme, and rosemary. Bring to boiling.

3. Roast, covered, 1¾ hours. Add potatoes and carrots. Roast, covered, about 45 minutes more or until meat and vegetables are tender. Transfer meat and vegetables to a platter; cover to keep warm.

4. For sauce, skim fat from cooking liquid; strain liquid through a fine-mesh sieve into a bowl. Return strained liquid to pot. Bring to boiling; reduce heat. Simmer, uncovered, 10 to 15 minutes or until slightly thickened. Serve sauce with meat and vegetables. Sprinkle with reserved bacon and, if desired, fresh thyme sprigs.

PER SERVING: 441 cal., 22 g fat (7 g sat. fat), 129 mg chol., 547 mg sodium, 15 g carb., 3 g fiber, 3 g sugars, 44 g pro.

tinga poblana

PREP: 30 minutes | **ROAST:** 1 hour 30 minutes at 325°F | **MAKES:** 8 servings (¾ cup each)

1 Tbsp. vegetable oil

1 2-lb. boneless pork shoulder, trimmed of fat and cut into 1-inch cubes

8 oz. uncooked chorizo sausage, casing removed

2 medium red potatoes, cut into ½-inch cubes (about 2 cups)

1 cup chopped onion

1 14.5-oz. can diced fire-roasted tomatoes, undrained

½ cup water

3 canned chipotle chile peppers in adobo sauce, chopped, plus 1 Tbsp. adobo sauce form the can (tip, *right*)

4 cloves garlic, minced

2 bay leaves

1 tsp. dried thyme, crushed

1 tsp. dried Mexican oregano, crushed

½ tsp. salt

¼ tsp. sugar

Tortilla chips or tortillas

2 avocados, halved, seeded, peeled, and thinly sliced

2 cups crumbled queso fresco (8 oz.)

1. Preheat oven to 325°F. In an oven-safe 6- to 8-qt. pot heat oil over medium-high heat. Add pork; cook and stir until browned. Remove pork from pot. Add chorizo to pot and cook over medium-high heat about 8 minutes or until well browned. Drain off fat.

2. Add pork and the next 11 ingredients (through sugar) to chorizo in pot. Roast, covered, 1½ to 2 hours or until pork and vegetables are tender. Discard bay leaves. Skim fat from cooking liquid. Serve with tortilla chips, avocado slices, and queso fresco.

SLOW COOKER DIRECTIONS: Brown pork and chorizo as directed in Step 1. In a 3½- or 4-qt. slow cooker combine pork, chorizo, and the next 11 ingredients (through sugar). Cover and cook on low 8 hours. Serve as directed in Step 2.

PER SERVING: *624 cal., 37 g fat (12 g sat. fat), 112 mg chol., 1,072 mg sodium, 36 g carb., 5 g fiber, 4 g sugars, 37 g pro.*

HOT STUFF!

Chile peppers contain oils that can irritate your skin and eyes. If your bare hands come in contact with the peppers, the tingling burn can last for hours even after washing your hands. Wear plastic or rubber gloves when working with chiles.

WHAT IS TINGA? THIS POPULAR MEXICAN DISH CONSISTS OF PORK BRAISED IN A SPICY CHILE SAUCE. IT CAN BE SERVED ON TOSTADAS, WITH TORTILLA CHIPS, AND IN TACOS.

wine-braised short ribs

PREP: 25 minutes | ROAST: 2 hours 30 minutes at 325°F | MAKES: 6 to 8 servings

6 to 8 bone-in beef short ribs (about 4 lb.)

1 tsp. kosher salt

¾ tsp. freshly ground black pepper

1 Tbsp. vegetable oil

4 large carrots, peeled and cut into chunks

2 stalks celery, cut into chunks

1 Tbsp. minced garlic

1 cup dry red wine (tip, *right*)

2 cups reduced-sodium beef broth

2 Tbsp. tomato paste

½ tsp. dried thyme, crushed

½ tsp. dried rosemary, crushed

1 14.4-oz. pkg. frozen pearl onions

Crusty bread

1. Preheat oven to 325°F. Sprinkle short ribs with salt and pepper. In an oven-safe 5- to 6-qt. pot heat oil over medium-high heat. Add ribs, in batches if necessary, and cook until browned on all sides. Remove ribs from pot and set aside. Measure 1 Tbsp. drippings and set aside; discard remaining drippings.

2. In the same pot cook carrots and celery in the reserved drippings over medium heat 5 minutes, stirring occasionally. Add garlic; cook and stir 1 minute more. Carefully add wine to pot. Cook and stir 5 minutes or until wine is reduced slightly, scraping up browned bits from the bottom of pot. Stir in broth, tomato paste, thyme, and rosemary until combined. Add ribs and pearl onions. Bring to boiling.

3. Roast, covered, 2½ to 3 hours or until ribs are tender. Use a slotted spoon to remove ribs and vegetables from braising liquid. Skim fat from braising liquid. Drizzle ribs and vegetables with some of the braising liquid. Serve with crusty bread.

PER SERVING: *906 cal., 56 g fat (23 g sat. fat), 211 mg chol., 903 mg sodium, 38 g carb., 5 g fiber, 9 g sugars, 55 g pro.*

IN THE RED

Red wine helps to tenderize the meat and adds richness and depth to the sauce. Reducing it in the pan before adding the other liquids allows most of the alcohol to evaporate. For the best flavor, be sure to choose a dry red wine, such as Cabernet, Merlot, or Pinot Noir.

brown ale–braised brisket

PREP: 30 minutes | **ROAST:** 3 hours 30 minutes at 325°F
MAKES: 10 to 12 servings (3 oz. meat + ½ cup vegetables + ¼ cup cooking liquid each)

1 3½- to 4-lb. flat-cut beef brisket, trimmed, leaving ¼-inch layer of fat

Salt and black pepper

1 Tbsp. vegetable oil

1 tsp. dried thyme, crushed

3 Tbsp. horseradish mustard or coarse-ground mustard

3 onions, cut into thick wedges

5 medium red potatoes (about 1½ lb.), halved, or 2 medium sweet potatoes, peeled and cut into quarters

1 large fennel bulb, trimmed, cored, and cut into thick wedges

4 cloves garlic, peeled and smashed

1 12-oz. bottle brown ale (such as Newcastle Brown Ale) or 1½ cups reduced-sodium beef broth

1 cup reduced-sodium beef broth

¼ cup tomato paste

1 tsp. orange zest

Crusty bread

1. Preheat oven to 325°F. Sprinkle brisket on both sides with salt and pepper. If necessary, cut brisket to fit in an oven-safe 6- to 8-qt. pot (tip, *below*). In the pot heat oil over medium-high heat. Add meat and cook until browned on both sides. Remove pot from heat; turn meat fat side up. Sprinkle with thyme and spread with mustard. Add onions, potatoes, fennel, and garlic to pot.

2. In a medium bowl whisk together ale, broth, tomato paste, and orange zest. Pour over meat. Bring to boiling.

3. Roast, covered, 3½ to 4 hours or until meat is fork-tender. Transfer meat to a cutting board. Transfer vegetables to a serving platter; cover to keep warm. Skim fat from cooking liquid; discard fat. Season cooking liquid to taste. Thinly slice meat across grain. Arrange on platter with vegetables and drizzle with some of the cooking liquid. Pass additional cooking liquid and serve with crusty bread.

PER SERVING: *568 cal., 30 g fat (11 g sat. fat), 137 mg chol., 660 mg sodium, 35 g carb., 4 g fiber, 6 g sugars, 34 g pro.*

THE RIGHT POT

When braising meat in liquids that contain acidic ingredients—such as tomatoes, wine, or vinegar—choose a Dutch oven with a stainless-steel, enamel, or nonstick interior. Other metallic surfaces can react with the acid, producing an unpleasant flavor. And in recipes that call for oven braising, such as this one, use a pot that is oven-safe.

dijon beef and mushrooms

PREP: 30 minutes | **ROAST:** 1 hour 30 minutes at 350°F | **MAKES:** 4 servings (1¼ cups each)

- 2 to 3 Tbsp. vegetable oil
- 2 8-oz. pkg. button and/or cremini mushrooms, quartered
- 1 cup chopped onion
- 3 cloves garlic, minced
- 1½ lb. boneless beef sirloin steak, cut into 1-inch pieces
- ½ tsp. salt
- ¼ tsp. black pepper
- ⅔ cup reduced-sodium beef broth
- ⅔ cup dry white wine
- 3 Tbsp. Dijon-style mustard
- 1 Tbsp. snipped fresh thyme or 1 tsp. dried thyme, crushed
- 2 Tbsp. butter, softened
- 2 Tbsp. all-purpose flour
  Garlic toasts or hot cooked pasta (optional)

1. Preheat oven to 350°F. In an oven-safe 5- to 6-qt. pot heat 1 Tbsp. of the oil over medium-high heat. Add mushrooms, onion, and garlic; cook and stir 6 minutes or until tender and beginning to brown. Remove mushroom mixture from pot.

2. Sprinkle meat with salt and pepper. In the same pot heat 1 Tbsp. oil over medium-high heat. Add half of the meat; cook until browned. Transfer to a bowl. Repeat with remaining meat, adding more oil if necessary. Return all the meat and the mushroom mixture to the pot. Add broth, wine, mustard, and dried thyme (if using). Bring to boiling, stirring to combine.

3. Roast, covered, 1 hour. In a small bowl stir together butter and flour. Stir butter mixture and fresh thyme (if using) into meat mixture in pot. Roast, covered, 30 minutes more or until meat is tender and sauce is slightly thickened. Serve meat mixture with garlic toasts or pasta and, if desired, fresh thyme sprigs.

TIP: For an easy side, serve a vegetable such as steamed French-cut green beans or a quick tossed salad.

PER SERVING: *533 cal., 33 g fat (12 g sat. fat), 141 mg chol., 747 mg sodium, 13 g carb., 2 g fiber, 5 g sugars, 39 g pro.*

IF YOUR FAMILY LIKES INTENSE MUSHROOM FLAVOR, CHOOSE CREMINI MUSHROOMS—ALSO KNOWN AS BABY PORTOBELLO MUSHROOMS—FOR THIS DISH. KEEP THE MUSHROOM FLAVOR ON THE MILD SIDE BY USING BUTTON MUSHROOMS.

| FAST PREP

pork pot roast in cider

PREP: 25 minutes | **COOK:** 1 hour 30 minutes | **MAKES:** 4 servings (5 oz. pork + ½ cup gravy each)

2   Tbsp. vegetable oil

1   1½- to 2-lb. boneless pork blade roast or sirloin roast, trimmed of fat

1¼ cups apple cider or apple juice

2   tsp. instant beef bouillon granules

½   tsp. dry mustard

¼   tsp. black pepper

3   medium red potatoes or round white potatoes, peeled (if desired) and quartered

3   medium carrots, cut into 2-inch pieces

3   medium parsnips, peeled and cut into 2-inch pieces

1   large onion, cut into wedges

⅓   cup cold water

¼   cup all-purpose flour

1. In a 4- to 6-qt. pot heat oil over medium-high heat. Add roast to pot and cook until browned on all sides. Drain off fat.

2. In a medium bowl stir together cider, bouillon granules, mustard, and pepper. Pour over meat in pot. Bring to boiling; reduce heat. Simmer, covered, 1 hour.

3. Add potatoes, carrots, parsnips, and onion to meat in pot. Simmer, covered, 30 to 40 minutes more or until meat and vegetables are tender. Transfer meat and vegetables to a serving platter, reserving juices in pot. Cover to keep warm.

4. For gravy, measure cooking juices; skim off fat. If necessary, add enough water to juices to equal 1½ cups. Return to pot. Stir the ⅓ cup cold water into the flour. Stir flour mixture into juices in pot. Cook and stir over medium heat until thickened and bubbly. Cook and stir 1 minute more. To serve, remove string from meat if present. Slice meat and serve with vegetables and gravy.

SLOW COOKER DIRECTIONS: Brown meat as directed in Step 1. In a 3½- or 4-qt. slow cooker layer potatoes, carrots, parsnips, and onion. Cut meat to fit if necessary; place on top of vegetables. Stir together cider, bouillon granules, mustard, and pepper. Pour over meat and vegetables in cooker. Cover and cook on low 8 to 10 hours or on high 4 to 5 hours or until tender. Transfer meat and vegetables to a serving platter; cover to keep warm. Continue as directed in Step 4.

PER SERVING: 765 cal., 49 g fat (15 g sat. fat), 123 mg chol., 573 mg sodium, 50 g carb., 6 g fiber, 15 g sugars, 32 g pro.

VARY THE VEGGIES

Change it up by substituting other root vegetables, such as rutabagas, turnips, or celery root, in place of the carrots and parsnips.

spicy spring picnic pork

PREP: 15 minutes | **SLOW COOK:** 8 to 10 hours (low) or 4 to 5 hours (high) | **MAKES:** 8 servings (1 sandwich each)

1   2- to 2½-lb. boneless pork shoulder, trimmed of fat

     Salt and black pepper

1   large sweet onion, cut into thin wedges

1   18- to 20-oz. bottle hot and spicy barbecue sauce (about 1¾ cups)

1   cup Dr Pepper carbonated beverage (not diet)

8   hamburger buns or 16 baguette slices, toasted

     Coleslaw (optional)

1. If necessary, cut meat to fit into a 3½- or 4-qt. slow cooker. Sprinkle meat with salt and pepper. Place onion wedges in the slow cooker; top with meat. In a medium bowl stir together barbecue sauce and carbonated beverage; pour over meat in cooker.

2. Cover and cook on low 8 to 10 hours or on high 4 to 5 hours. Transfer meat to a cutting board. Shred meat using two forks. With a slotted spoon, remove the onions from the cooking liquid and add to meat. Pour cooking liquid from slow cooker into a glass measuring cup or bowl; skim fat from cooking liquid. Return pork and onions to slow cooker; add enough cooking liquid to moisten meat mixture.

3. To serve, use a slotted spoon to spoon meat mixture and, if desired, coleslaw into buns.

PER SERVING: *378 cal., 8 g fat (3 g sat. fat), 73 mg chol., 1,355 mg sodium, 45 g carb., 1 g fiber, 21 g sugars, 27 g pro.*

SLOW COOKER SHOPPING

Slow cooker options are endless—sizes, colors, patterns, and an array of features to make your cooking experience easier. If you're in the market for a new cooker, consider some of these features.

* Touch and Go: User-friendly control panels allow you to program cook times, and the cooker switches to warm setting when the time's up.

* Potluck Partner: If you like to take your slow cooker on the go, look for secure clip-lock gasket lids, full-grip handles, and clip-on spoon options. Slow cookers with these options make toting a breeze.

* Stir It Up: Some slow cookers even stir themselves! To prevent losing heat every time you open the lid to stir, search for a brand with a built-in paddle that rotates every 30 minutes.

* Taskmaster: The one-trick slow cooker is a thing of the past. Now you can find cookers that do it all—sauté, slow cook, and steam options all in one pot so you can bypass any stove-top browning! For more multiuse cookers, check out the pressure cookers on *page 218*.

chicken and baby potatoes with pesto

PREP: 20 minutes | **SLOW COOK:** 6 to 8 hours (low) or 3 to 4 hours (high)
MAKES: 5 servings (4 oz. chicken + ¾ cup potato mixture each)

1 **lb. red new potatoes, halved**

1 **medium onion, cut into wedges**

3 **cloves garlic, minced**

1 **sprig fresh rosemary**

1 **lemon**

2 **chicken breast halves with bone (about 2½ lb. total)**

½ **cup reduced-sodium chicken broth**

¼ **tsp. salt**

⅛ **tsp. black pepper**

2 **Tbsp. refrigerated basil pesto**

¼ **cup finely shredded Parmesan cheese (1 oz.)**

1. In a 4- to 5-qt. slow cooker place the first four ingredients (through rosemary). Use a vegetable peeler to peel long strips of zest from the lemon. Add lemon zest to cooker. Cut remaining lemon into wedges and set aside. Place chicken in cooker; add broth. Cover and cook on low 6 to 8 hours or on high 3 to 4 hours or until chicken is done (170°F) and potatoes are tender.

2. Transfer chicken to a platter; remove and discard skin and bone. Slice chicken breasts. Using a slotted spoon, transfer potato mixture to the platter. Discard rosemary and lemon zest. Sprinkle chicken and potato mixture with salt and pepper. In a bowl stir together pesto and 1 Tbsp. of the cooking liquid; discard remaining cooking liquid. Drizzle chicken and potato mixture with pesto mixture. Sprinkle with Parmesan cheese. Serve with lemon wedges and, if desired, additional lemon zest.

PER SERVING: *307 cal., 8 g fat (2 g sat. fat), 114 mg chol., 406 mg sodium, 18 g carb., 2 g fiber, 3 g sugars, 38 g pro.*

| FAST PREP

shredded chicken tacos with fire-roasted tomato sauce

PREP: 25 minutes | **COOK:** 35 minutes | **MAKES:** 8 servings (2 tacos each)

- 1 Tbsp. vegetable oil
- 2 lb. skinless, boneless chicken thighs
- 1 14.5-oz. can fire-roasted diced tomatoes, undrained
- 1 fresh jalapeño chile pepper, stem removed and halved (tip, *page 14*)
- 3 cloves garlic, peeled
- 2 Tbsp. ground ancho chile pepper, chili powder, or chipotle chile pepper (tip, *right*)
- 1 Tbsp. ground cumin
- ½ tsp. salt
- 16 6-inch corn or flour tortillas, warmed

  Guacamole, pico de gallo, snipped fresh cilantro, sliced radishes, and/or lime wedges (optional)

1. In a 4- to 6-qt. pot heat oil over medium heat. Brown the chicken thighs, half at a time, in the hot oil, turning once. Return all the chicken to the pot. Meanwhile, for sauce, in a blender combine the next six ingredients (through salt); cover and blend until smooth. Pour sauce over chicken in pot. Bring to boiling; reduce heat. Simmer, covered, about 35 minutes or until chicken is very tender.

2. Transfer chicken to a bowl. Shred chicken using two forks. Add sauce from pot to shredded chicken to moisten. Serve chicken in tortillas with, if desired, guacamole, pico de gallo, cilantro, radishes, and/or lime wedges.

SLOW COOKER DIRECTIONS: Prepare sauce as directed; pour into a 3½- or 4-qt. slow cooker. Add chicken thighs; stir to coat. Cover and cook on low 5 to 6 hours or on high 2½ to 3 hours. Continue as directed in Step 2.

PER SERVING: *271 cal., 8 g fat (1 g sat. fat), 106 mg chol., 414 mg sodium, 24 g carb., 4 g fiber, 4 g sugars, 25 g pro.*

HEAT BOOSTER

For more heat and a hit of smoky flavor, use ground chipotle chile pepper instead of ancho chile pepper in the sauce.

moroccan tagine-style chicken thighs

PREP: 20 minutes | **ROAST:** 1 hour at 350°F | **MAKES:** 6 to 8 servings (2 thighs + ⅔ cup fruit each)

4	tsp. ground cinnamon
1½	tsp. caraway seeds, crushed
1½	tsp. ground cumin
1½	tsp. ground cardamom
⅛	to ¼ tsp. cayenne pepper
8	cloves garlic, minced
12	chicken thighs, skinned (4 to 5 lb. total)
2	Tbsp. olive oil
1	14.5-oz. can reduced-sodium chicken broth
1	cup dried apricots, quartered
1	cup pitted dates, quartered
¼	cup sliced almonds, ground
1	tsp. ground turmeric
¾	tsp. salt
¼	tsp. black pepper
¼	tsp. saffron threads, crushed
⅓	cup snipped fresh cilantro
2	Tbsp. sliced almonds, toasted (tip, *right*)
	Hot cooked couscous or rice (optional)

1. Preheat oven to 350°F. In a small bowl combine the first six ingredients (through garlic). Sprinkle spice mixture over chicken and rub in with your fingers.

2. In an oven-safe 6- to 8-qt. pot heat oil over medium-high heat. Brown chicken, half at a time, in the hot oil about 6 minutes, turning once.

3. Add the next eight ingredients (through saffron). Roast, covered, 1 hour or until chicken is tender.

4. Use a slotted spoon to transfer chicken mixture to a shallow serving dish (some meat may fall off the bone). Sprinkle chicken with cilantro and sliced almonds. Skim fat from cooking liquid. Serve chicken with cooking liquid and, if desired, couscous.

SLOW COOKER DIRECTIONS: Prepare as directed in Steps 1 and 2. Place chicken in a 6- to 7-qt. slow cooker. In a medium bowl combine broth, apricots, dates, ground almonds, turmeric, salt, pepper, and saffron; pour over chicken. Cover and cook on low 8 hours or on high 4 hours. Continue as directed in Step 4.

PER SERVING: *501 cal., 17 g fat (3 g sat. fat), 213 mg chol., 627 mg sodium, 41 g carb., 6 g fiber, 31 g sugars, 49 g pro.*

ROASTY TOASTY

To toast nuts, spread nuts in a shallow baking pan. Bake 5 to 10 minutes in a 350°F oven or until light brown, watching carefully and stirring once or twice. Toast finely chopped or ground nuts in a dry skillet over medium heat. Stir often so they don't burn.

Mediterranean Steamed
Mussels and Clams, *page 50*

around
the world

Who needs takeout when global cuisine is this simple to make? These weeknight-friendly recipes capture the cultural flavors you love, including Chinese, Mediterranean, Mexican, and more.

spicy chinese chicken and noodles

PREP: 20 minutes | **COOK:** 13 minutes | **MAKES:** 6 servings (1 cup each)

2 tsp. vegetable oil

1½ lb. skinless, boneless chicken breast halves, cut into 1-inch pieces

3 cups reduced-sodium chicken broth

2 Tbsp. reduced-sodium soy sauce

2 Tbsp. rice vinegar

1 Tbsp. honey

1 Tbsp. Asian chile paste (sambal oelek)

1 Tbsp. sriracha sauce

4 cloves garlic, minced

4 dried red chiles

8 to 10 oz. dried Chinese noodles, broken

1 Tbsp. rice wine or dry sherry

⅓ cup sliced green onions

⅓ cup chopped peanuts

1. In a 4-qt. pot heat oil over medium-high heat. Add chicken; cook and stir until browned. Add the next seven ingredients (through garlic); whisk to combine. Stir in the dried red chiles. Bring to boiling; reduce heat. Simmer, covered, 10 minutes, stirring occasionally.

2. Remove and discard chiles. Return chicken mixture to boiling; stir in noodles. Reduce heat. Simmer, uncovered, 3 minutes or until noodles are tender, stirring occasionally. Remove from heat. Stir in rice wine. Sprinkle with green onions and chopped peanuts. If desired, serve with additional sriracha sauce.

PER SERVING: *404 cal., 15 g fat (5 g sat. fat), 83 mg chol., 748 mg sodium, 32 g carb., 2 g fiber, 6 g sugars, 34 g pro.*

szechwan chicken

PREP: 20 minutes | **COOK:** 10 minutes | **MAKES:** 6 servings (1 cup chicken mixture + 1 cup rice each)

1 Tbsp. vegetable oil

1 lb. skinless, boneless chicken thighs, cut into ½-inch pieces

1 cup thinly sliced carrots

1 cup thinly sliced celery

1 13- to 14-oz. can (8 oz. drained weight) straw mushrooms or mushroom stems and pieces, drained

1 15-oz. can (7 oz. drained weight) whole baby corn, drained and cut up

⅔ cup bottled stir-fry sauce

1 Tbsp. chili bean sauce (tip, *right*)

2 8.8-oz. pouches cooked brown or white rice, heated according to package directions

¼ cup honey dry-roasted peanuts, coarsely chopped (optional)

1. In a 3- to 4-qt. pot heat oil over medium-high heat. Add chicken; cook and stir about 5 minutes or until browned.

2. Add the next six ingredients (through bean sauce) to chicken in pot; stir to combine. Bring to boiling; reduce heat. Simmer, covered, 8 minutes. Uncover; simmer 2 minutes more or until chicken is cooked through and vegetables are tender. Serve with hot cooked rice and sprinkle with peanuts.

TO MAKE AHEAD: Prepare as directed, except do not heat rice. Place chicken mixture in an airtight container. Cover and store up to 3 days in the refrigerator. To serve, reheat chicken mixture in the pot, covered, over medium heat. Prepare rice and serve as directed.

PER SERVING: 289 cal., 10 g fat (1 g sat. fat), 71 mg chol., 1,053 mg sodium, 31 g carb., 4 g fiber, 3 g sugars, 21 g pro.

SPICY SZECHWAN

Szechwan- and Hunan-style cuisines are known for being hot and spicy. Chili bean sauce provides the spice in this dish. Look for it in the Asian section of your supermarket or at Asian foods stores.

chinese congee with ginger and chicken

PREP: 20 minutes | **COOK:** 1 hour 15 minutes | **MAKES:** 4 servings (1¾ cups each)

1½ lb. skinless, boneless chicken thighs, cut into 1-inch pieces

4 cups reduced-sodium chicken broth

1 cup uncooked regular brown rice

½ cup chopped onion

3 Tbsp. minced fresh ginger

1 Tbsp. minced garlic

⅛ tsp. black pepper

Toppings such as bottled hot pepper sauce, bottled ponzu sauce, sliced green onions, chopped peanuts, snipped fresh basil, and/or reduced-sodium soy sauce

1. In a 3- to 4-qt. pot combine the first seven ingredients (through black pepper). Bring to boiling; reduce heat. Simmer, covered, about 1¼ hours or until mixture reaches a porridgelike consistency, stirring occasionally. Spoon congee into bowls and serve with toppings.

PER SERVING: 423 cal., 9 g fat (2 g sat. fat), 160 mg chol., 888 mg sodium, 41 g carb., 2 g fiber, 2 g sugars, 41 g pro.

WHAT IS CONGEE?

A popular breakfast dish in China, congee is a porridge made from rice that serves as the base for various proteins, including fish, chicken, and eggs.

easy chicken korma

PREP: 35 minutes | **COOK:** 30 minutes | **MAKES:** 6 servings (1 cup korma + ½ cup rice each)

1 Tbsp. vegetable oil

3 lb. skinless, boneless chicken thighs, cut into 1½-inch pieces

2 medium sweet potatoes, cut into 1-inch pieces

1 large onion, thinly sliced

1 14-oz. can unsweetened coconut milk

¾ cup chicken broth

2 Tbsp. tomato paste

1 Tbsp. grated fresh ginger

1 Tbsp. garam masala

2 tsp. ground turmeric

2 tsp. chili powder

1 tsp. salt

3 cloves garlic, minced

⅓ cup ground almonds or almond meal

¼ cup plain Greek yogurt

Hot cooked rice

1. In a 4- to 5-qt. pot heat half of the oil over medium-high heat. Add half of the chicken; cook and stir until browned. Remove chicken from pot. Repeat with remaining chicken and oil. Return all the chicken to the pot. Stir in the next 11 ingredients (through garlic). Bring to boiling; reduce heat. Simmer, covered, 30 minutes or until sweet potatoes are tender.

2. Before serving, stir in ground almonds and yogurt. Serve over hot cooked rice.

PER SERVING: 641 cal., 26 g fat (13 g sat. fat), 215 mg chol., 1,236 mg sodium, 46 g carb., 4 g fiber, 6 g sugars, 51 g pro.

WHAT IS KORMA?

A popular dish in India and Pakistan, korma consists of meat and/or vegetables braised in a spicy curry sauce. It's traditionally served with fragrant basmati rice.

asian short ribs

PREP: 30 minutes | **ROAST:** 2 hours 45 minutes at 350°F | **MAKES:** 6 to 8 servings

2½ cups reduced-sodium beef broth

¾ cup hoisin sauce

3 Tbsp. reduced-sodium soy sauce

2 tsp. toasted sesame oil (tip, *right*)

1½ tsp. Chinese five-spice powder

⅛ tsp. cayenne pepper (optional)

3½ to 4 lb. beef short ribs, trimmed of fat and cut into serving-size pieces

¼ tsp. black pepper

1 Tbsp. vegetable oil

½ cup chopped onion

3 to 4 cloves garlic, minced

1 tsp. grated fresh ginger

1½ cups sliced fresh shiitake mushrooms, stems removed, or sliced fresh button mushrooms

Hot cooked rice (optional)

Green onions, bias-sliced into 1-inch pieces (optional)

1. Preheat oven to 350°F. In a medium bowl combine the first six ingredients (through cayenne pepper); set aside. Sprinkle ribs with black pepper. In an oven-safe 4- to 5-qt. pot heat oil over medium-high heat. Add ribs, half at a time, and cook until browned on all sides. Remove ribs.

2. Add onion, garlic, and ginger to pot. Cook and stir 1 to 2 minutes or until onion is lightly browned. Return ribs to pot; add broth mixture. Bring to boiling.

3. Roast, covered, 2 hours, stirring once or twice. Stir in mushrooms. Roast, covered, about 45 minutes more or until ribs are tender. Transfer ribs to a deep platter; cover to keep warm.

4. For sauce, pour cooking liquid into a large glass measuring cup; skim off fat. Return liquid to pot. Bring to boiling. Cook, uncovered, 2 to 3 minutes or until slightly thickened. Pour some of the sauce over ribs and pass remaining sauce. If desired, serve ribs with rice and sprinkle with green onions.

PER SERVING: *316 cal., 16 g fat (5 g sat. fat), 65 mg chol., 1,044 mg sodium, 18 g carb., 1 g fiber, 10 g sugars, 24 g pro.*

SMART SHOPPING

Look for hoisin sauce, toasted sesame oil, and Chinese five-spice powder in the Asian foods section of your supermarket or at Asian foods stores. To get the richest flavor, be sure to use dark-color toasted sesame oil rather than the light-color sesame oil, which has not been toasted.

| FAST PREP | CALORIE SMART

miso hot pot

START TO FINISH: 35 minutes | **MAKES:** 6 servings (1¾ cups each)

- 4 tsp. canola oil
- 12 oz. boneless pork loin roast, trimmed of fat and cut into 1-inch cubes
- ¾ cup chopped red sweet pepper
- ½ cup chopped onion
- 1 Tbsp. grated fresh ginger
- 2 cloves garlic, minced
- ¼ tsp. black pepper
- 8 cups water
- ¼ cup red miso paste
- 1 10- to 12-oz. pkg. frozen shelled edamame
- 4 cups thinly sliced savoy cabbage
- 2 to 3 medium radishes, very thinly sliced

1. In a 4-qt. pot heat 2 tsp. of the oil over medium-high heat. Add pork; cook until browned, stirring occasionally. Remove pork. Drain off any fat.

2. In the same pot cook sweet pepper and onion in the remaining 2 tsp. oil over medium heat 5 minutes, stirring occasionally. Add ginger, garlic, and black pepper; cook and stir 30 seconds more. Add 7 cups of the water. In a bowl gradually whisk the remaining 1 cup water into the miso paste. Add to pot and bring to boiling.

3. Add edamame and the pork. Return to boiling; reduce heat. Simmer, covered, 3 minutes. Stir in cabbage. Cook 2 minutes more, stirring occasionally. Serve topped with radish slices.

PER SERVING: 216 cal., 9 g fat (1 g sat. fat), 39 mg chol., 486 mg sodium, 14 g carb., 5 g fiber, 6 g sugars, 20 g pro.

ALL ABOUT MISO

This protein-rich Japanese staple is a fermented soybean paste that adds an intense, savory flavor to foods. Miso is a good source of essential minerals, folic acid, B vitamins, and vitamins E and K. Most commonly found in red and white varieties, miso is in the natural foods section of large supermarkets or at Asian foods stores.

mexican carnitas

PREP: 30 minutes | **COOK:** 2 hours 15 minutes | **MAKES:** 10 servings (½ cup each)

2 Tbsp. vegetable oil

3 lb. boneless pork shoulder roast, trimmed of fat and cut into 1½-inch pieces

⅓ cup chopped onion

3 cloves garlic, minced

1 orange

2 cups water

4 sprigs fresh thyme

1 tsp. salt

1 tsp. dried Mexican oregano or regular oregano, crushed

½ tsp. crushed red pepper

2 bay leaves

Flour tortillas (optional)

Lime wedges (optional)

Sliced fresh jalapeño chile peppers (optional) (tip, page 14)

Guacamole (optional)

1. In a 4-qt. pot heat oil over medium-high heat. Brown meat, half at a time, in the hot oil, stirring to brown evenly. Remove meat from pot. Add onion and garlic to pot and cook until lightly browned and tender. Return meat to pot.

2. Remove 1 tsp. zest and squeeze ⅓ cup juice from orange. Add the orange zest and juice and the next six ingredients (through bay leaves) to pot. Bring to boiling; reduce heat. Simmer, covered, 2 hours. Remove lid; increase heat so mixture boils gently. Cook, uncovered, 15 to 20 minutes or until nearly all of the liquid has evaporated, gently stirring occasionally. Discard thyme sprigs and bay leaves.

3. Use a slotted spoon to transfer meat to a serving bowl. If desired, serve on tortillas with lime wedges, chile peppers, and guacamole.

TO MAKE AHEAD: Prepare carnitas as directed. Transfer carnitas to an airtight container; cool slightly. Cover and store in the refrigerator up to 3 days or freeze up to 3 months. To serve, thaw carnitas overnight in the refrigerator if frozen. Reheat in a heavy pot over medium heat, stirring occasionally, or heat in a slow cooker on high 2 hours.

PER SERVING: 204 cal., 7 g fat (2 g sat. fat), 84 mg chol., 307 mg sodium, 2 g carb., 0 g fiber, 1 g sugars, 31 g pro.

IN SPANISH, "CARNITAS" MEANS "LITTLE MEATS." USED AS A FILLING FOR TACOS OR BURRITOS, CARNITAS IS SIMPLY SMALL SHREDS OF WELL-BROWNED, SEASONED MEAT.

arroz con albóndigas

PREP: 20 minutes | **COOK:** 20 minutes | **MAKES:** 6 to 8 servings (1½ cups each)

- 1 14.4-oz. pkg. frozen yellow, green, and red sweet peppers and onions stir-fry vegetables or two 8-oz. pkg. frozen chopped green sweet peppers and onions
- 1 14.5-oz. can diced tomatoes with Italian herbs, undrained
- 1½ cups water
- 1 cup converted rice
- 1 cup frozen peas*
- ½ cup pitted green olives, halved
- 2 Tbsp. tomato paste
- 2 tsp. ground cumin
- 2 tsp. paprika
- ½ tsp. salt
- ⅛ tsp. black pepper
- 1 14-oz. pkg. frozen meatballs (about 26)
  Bottled hot pepper sauce or salsa (optional)

1. In a 4- to 5-qt. pot combine the first 11 ingredients (through black pepper). Top with meatballs. Bring to boiling over medium-high heat; reduce heat to low. Simmer, covered, 20 minutes or until rice is cooked through, meatballs are heated through, and most of the liquid is absorbed. If desired, serve with hot pepper sauce.

*TIP: For brighter color, add peas the last 2 minutes of cooking.

PER SERVING: 401 cal., 19 g fat (7 g sat. fat), 23 mg chol., 1,172 mg sodium, 43 g carb., 4 g fiber, 8 g sugars, 14 g pro.

IN A NAME

In Spanish, "arroz con albóndigas" means "rice with meatballs." This quick version of the traditional Mexican dish calls for purchased meatballs and parboiled rice.

aguadito de pollo (peruvian chicken soup)

PREP: 15 minutes | **COOK:** 30 minutes | **MAKES:** 6 to 8 servings (2 cups each)

2 Tbsp. olive oil

1 lb. skinless, boneless chicken breast halves

2 medium carrots, halved lengthwise and thinly sliced crosswise

1 medium green sweet pepper, cut into thin bite-size strips

½ cup chopped onion

6 cups reduced-sodium chicken broth

8 oz. round red potatoes, cut into 1-inch cubes

½ cup quinoa, rinsed and drained

2 medium ears fresh sweet corn or 1 cup frozen whole kernel corn, thawed

1 recipe Cilantro Oil (optional)

Lime wedges

1. In a 6- to 8-qt. pot heat 1 Tbsp. of the oil over medium-high heat. Add chicken; cook 6 to 8 minutes or until lightly browned, turning once. Remove chicken and set aside. Add carrots, sweet pepper, onion, and the remaining 1 Tbsp. oil to the skillet. Cook 5 to 7 minutes or until vegetables begin to brown, stirring occasionally. Add broth, potatoes, and quinoa. Return chicken to pot. Bring to boiling; reduce heat. Simmer, covered, 10 minutes.

2. Meanwhile, husk and clean fresh sweet corn (if using). Cut ears crosswise into 2-inch slices.

3. Check chicken for doneness. If no longer pink (170°F), transfer chicken to a cutting board. (If still pink, leave in the pot.) Add sliced ears of corn (or 1 cup thawed frozen corn) to the pot. Return to boiling; reduce heat. Simmer, covered, 5 minutes more or until potatoes and corn are tender and chicken is no longer pink (if still in the pot).

4. Coarsely shred chicken using two forks. Add shredded chicken and, if desired, the Cilantro Oil to the soup. Cook over low heat 2 to 3 minutes to heat through. Serve soup with lime wedges.

PER SERVING: 391 cal., 19 g fat (3 g sat. fat), 55 mg chol., 719 mg sodium, 31 g carb., 4 g fiber, 6 g sugars, 25 g pro.

CILANTRO OIL: In a food processor or blender combine 3 cups packed fresh cilantro (tough stems removed); ¼ cup olive oil; 2 Tbsp. lime juice; 4 cloves garlic, sliced; ½ tsp. crushed red pepper; and ¼ tsp. salt. Cover and process or blend until smooth, scraping sides of bowl as needed.

CHICKEN SOUP FROM PERU

Although there are many variations of this South American comfort food, most include quinoa, potatoes, and corn, which are staples of this region.

FROM THE WESTERN PYRENEES REGION OF FRANCE AND SPAIN, THIS BRAISED CHICKEN IS PREPARED IN THE BASQUE STYLE, WHICH USUALLY INCLUDES TOMATOES, SWEET PEPPERS, AND OLIVES.

basque chicken

START TO FINISH: 30 minutes | **MAKES:** 6 servings (1½ cups each)

1¼ lb. skinless, boneless chicken thighs, cut into 2-inch pieces

½ tsp. salt

¼ tsp. black pepper

1 Tbsp. olive oil

1 onion, thinly sliced

1 red sweet pepper, cut into ¼-inch-thick strips

2 cloves garlic, minced

12 oz. red potatoes, cut into ½-inch-wide wedges and halved crosswise

1 14.5-oz. can diced tomatoes, drained

1 cup chicken broth

¼ tsp. dried thyme, crushed

½ tsp. dried savory, crushed

⅓ cup small pimiento-stuffed olives

1. Sprinkle chicken with ¼ tsp. of the salt and the black pepper. In a 5- to 6-qt. pot heat oil over medium-high heat. Add chicken; cook about 4 minutes or until lightly browned, turning to brown evenly.

2. Add onion and sweet pepper to chicken in pot; cook 3 minutes or until crisp-tender. Add garlic; cook 30 seconds more. Add the next five ingredients (through savory) and the remaining ¼ tsp. salt. Bring to boiling; reduce heat. Simmer, covered, about 20 minutes or until chicken and potatoes are tender. Remove from heat. Stir in olives.

SLOW COOKER DIRECTIONS: Prepare as directed through Step 1. In a 3½- or 4-qt. slow cooker combine chicken, onion, sweet pepper, and potatoes. Stir in tomatoes, broth, garlic, thyme, savory, ¼ tsp. salt, and the black pepper. Cover and cook on low 10 to 11 hours or on high 5 to 5½ hours. Stir in olives and, if desired, top with additional fresh thyme.

PER SERVING: *204 cal., 6 g fat (1 g sat. fat), 79 mg chol., 576 mg sodium, 16 g carb., 3 g fiber, 5 g sugars, 21 g pro.*

mediterranean steamed mussels and clams

PREP: 20 minutes | **SOAK:** 45 minutes | **COOK:** 11 minutes
MAKES: 12 servings (7 shellfish + ¼ cup broth each)

2 lb. fresh mussels in shells

2 lb. fresh littleneck clams in shells

¼ cup butter, softened

2 Tbsp. snipped fresh parsley

1 Tbsp. snipped fresh tarragon or thyme

1 clove garlic, minced

½ tsp. salt

¼ tsp. black pepper

1 Tbsp. olive oil

1 bulb fennel, trimmed and finely chopped

½ cup finely chopped onion

4 cloves garlic, thinly sliced

2 cups white wine or dry vermouth

1 cup chopped tomatoes

1 Tbsp. fresh lemon juice

Toasted bread slices (optional)

1. To clean live mussels and clams, scrub under cold running water. If necessary, remove beards from mussels (tip, *below*). In an 8-qt. pot combine 4 qt. cold water and ⅓ cup salt; add mussels and clams. Soak 15 minutes; drain and rinse. Discard water. Repeat soaking, draining, and rinsing twice.

2. In a small bowl combine the next six ingredients (thorugh pepper). Use a fork or the back of a spoon to work herbs into butter.

3. In a heavy 8-qt. pot with a tight-fitting lid heat oil over medium-high heat. Add fennel, onion, and the sliced garlic; cook and stir 5 minutes or until onion is tender. Stir in wine; bring to boiling. Immediately add mussels and clams. Cover tightly and cook undisturbed 2 minutes.

4. Lift lid and, working quickly to retain as much heat in the pot as possible, stir in the herbed butter, tomatoes, and lemon juice. Cook, covered, over high heat 4 to 6 minutes more or just until shells open.

5. Using a slotted spoon, scoop shellfish into a serving bowl. Discard any mussels or clams that do not open. Pour the cooking liquid over shellfish. Serve immediately with toasted bread for sopping up the liquid.

PER SERVING: 417 cal., 20 g fat (5 g sat. fat), 59 mg chol, 1,125 mg sodium, 26 g carb., 2 g fiber, 2 g sugars, 25 g pro.

SHELLFISH PRIMER

When purchasing shellfish, look for shells that are tightly closed—this indicates the shellfish is still alive. Mussels might gape slightly but should close when tapped. To remove the beard (the small stringy fibers between the shells), grasp it firmly and tug it back and forth. Mussels are often sold debearded.

 | FAST PREP

bayou gumbo

PREP: 20 minutes | **COOK:** 30 minutes | **MAKES:** 6 to 8 servings (1⅓ cups gumbo + ½ cup rice each)

⅓ cup all-purpose flour

⅓ cup vegetable oil

1 cup chopped onion

½ cup chopped celery

½ cup chopped green sweet pepper

½ cup chopped red sweet pepper

2 cloves garlic, minced

3 cups reduced-sodium chicken broth

2 cups sliced okra or one 10-oz. pkg. frozen sliced okra

¼ tsp. black pepper

⅛ tsp. cayenne pepper

12 oz. cooked andouille sausage or smoked sausage, sliced

1 lb. fresh peeled and deveined medium shrimp, rinsed and patted dry

¼ cup chopped green onions

Hot cooked rice (tip, *right*)

1. For roux, in a 6-qt. heavy pot stir together flour and oil until smooth. Cook and stir constantly over medium-high heat about 5 minutes or until the roux is dark reddish brown.

2. Stir in the next five ingredients (through garlic). Cook 5 minutes or until vegetables are tender, stirring frequently. Add broth, okra, black pepper, and cayenne pepper. Simmer, covered, 15 minutes, stirring occasionally.

3. Stir in sausage; heat through. Add shrimp and green onions; cook 2 to 4 minutes or until shrimp are opaque, stirring frequently. Serve over rice.

PER SERVING: *460 cal., 22 g fat (5 g sat. fat), 122 mg chol., 870 mg sodium, 35 g carb., 3 g fiber, 3 g sugars, 30 g pro.*

RICE ALONG

Rice goes with gumbo so well because it soaks up the saucy broth of the thick Creole stew. Skip a step and buy packages of microwave-ready rice to heat up just before dinner's done. Or skip the rice and serve with thick slices of buttered bread.

 | FAST PREP

low-country shrimp boil

PREP: 15 minutes | **SLOW COOK:** 7 to 8 hours (low) or 3½ to 4 hours (high) + 10 minutes (high)
MAKES: 6 servings (2 cups each)

4   cups reduced-sodium chicken broth or water

1   lb. tiny red or yellow new potatoes

14   to 16 oz. cooked andouille or kielbasa sausage, cut into 1½-inch pieces

½   cup frozen small whole onions, thawed

½   to 1 Tbsp. Old Bay seasoning or crab and shrimp boil seasoning

¼   to ½ tsp. cayenne pepper

3   ears fresh sweet corn, husks and silks removed and cut crosswise into fourths

1½   lb. fresh or frozen large shrimp in shells (thawed if frozen), rinsed and patted dry

2   Tbsp. butter, melted

Hot sauce

1. In a 6- to 7-qt. slow cooker combine the first six ingredients (through cayenne pepper). Place corn on top of the potato mixture. Cover and cook on low 7 to 8 hours or on high 3½ to 4 hours or or until corn and potatoes are just tender.

2. If using low, turn cooker to high. Gently stir the shrimp into the potato mixture. Cover and cook 10 minutes more or until shrimp are opaque.

3. Using a slotted spoon, transfer shrimp mixture to an extra-large bowl. Pour butter over shrimp mixture; toss gently to coat. Spoon some of the cooking liquid over the mixture. Serve with hot sauce.

TIP: For easy cleanup, line your slow cooker with a disposable slow cooker liner. Add ingredients as directed in recipe. Once your dish is finished cooking, spoon the food out of your slow cooker and simply dispose of the liner. Do not lift or transport the disposable liner with food inside.

PER SERVING: *416 cal., 16 g fat (6 g sat. fat), 193 mg chol., 1,583 mg sodium, 31 g carb., 3 g fiber, 8 g sugars, 39 g pro.*

Beefy Chili Mac, *page 68*

noodles, noodles, noodles

When you need a dinner the whole family will get excited about, bring on the noodles! Here you'll find recipes that will satisfy every palate—Thai-style chicken and noodles, slow-cooker baked ziti, and more.

beef stroganoff hot pot

PREP: 20 minutes | **COOK:** 30 minutes | **MAKES:** 6 servings (1⅓ cups each)

1 lb. beef sirloin steak, trimmed of fat

Salt and black pepper

2 Tbsp. butter

8 oz. fresh button mushrooms, sliced

1 cup chopped onion

2 cloves garlic, minced

5 cups reduced-sodium beef broth

1 Tbsp. Worcestershire sauce

1 Tbsp. tomato paste

1½ cups dried egg noodles

½ cup sour cream

2 Tbsp. all-purpose flour

Snipped fresh Italian parsley

1. Sprinkle meat with salt and pepper; slice into bite-size pieces. In a 5- to 6-qt. pot melt butter over medium-high heat. Cook steak, half at a time, in the hot butter until browned. Remove meat from pot.

2. Add mushrooms, onion, and garlic to the pot. Cook and stir over medium heat 5 to 7 minutes or until mushrooms are tender. Stir in broth, Worcestershire sauce, and tomato paste; bring to boiling. Add noodles; boil gently, uncovered, 5 to 7 minutes or until noodles are tender.

3. In a medium bowl whisk together the ½ cup sour cream and the flour. Whisk a cup of the broth from the pot into the sour cream mixture until smooth. Return sour cream mixture to pot. Cook and stir until thickened and bubbly. Cook and stir 1 minute more. Add meat; cook just until meat is heated though. Top servings with parsley and, if desired, additional sour cream.

PER SERVING: *248 cal., 11 g fat (6 g sat. fat), 72 mg chol., 565 mg sodium, 15 g carb., 1 g fiber, 4 g sugars, 22 g pro.*

beefy french onion noodle pot

START TO FINISH: 1 hour | **MAKES:** 6 servings (1⅓ cups each)

¼ cup vegetable oil

2 cups sliced fresh mushrooms

3 cups thinly sliced onions

10 oz. beef sirloin, trimmed of fat and cut into very thin strips

Salt and black pepper

2 32-oz. boxes reduced-sodium beef broth

⅓ cup dry white wine (optional)

1 Tbsp. Worcestershire sauce

¼ tsp. freshly ground black pepper

4 oz. very wide homestyle egg noodles, broken if long

Cheesy Bread (optional)

1. In a 5- to 6-qt. pot heat 1 Tbsp. of the oil over medium-high heat. Add mushrooms and cook until softened, stirring occasionally. Add onions and an additional 1 Tbsp. oil; cook and stir over medium heat until mushrooms and onions are lightly browned. Reduce heat to low. Cook, covered, 10 minutes or until soft and golden, stirring if necessary. Remove mushrooms and onions from pot.

2. Sprinkle beef strips with salt and pepper. Heat the remaining 2 Tbsp. oil in the same pot over medium-high heat. Add beef; cook and stir until browned. Remove beef from pot. Stir in broth, wine (if using), Worcestershire sauce, and freshly ground pepper. Bring to boiling; add noodles, mushrooms, and onions. Cook, uncovered, according to package directions for noodles, adding the meat the last 3 minutes of cooking. If desired, top servings with Cheesy Bread.

PER SERVING: 275 cal., 12 g fat (2 g sat. fat), 44 mg chol., 664 mg sodium, 24 g carb., 2 g fiber, 6 g sugars, 18 g pro.

CHEESY BREAD: Preheat broiler. Arrange 6 slices toasted French bread on a baking sheet and sprinkle with shredded Swiss cheese. Broil 3 to 4 inches from the heat 1 minute or until cheese melts and lightly browns.

beef goulash

PREP: 25 minutes | **COOK:** 15 minutes | **MAKES:** 4 servings (1½ cups each)

8 oz. boneless beef top sirloin
   steak, trimmed of fat
   Salt and black pepper

1 tsp. olive oil

¾ cup thinly sliced carrots

½ cup chopped onion

2 cloves garlic, minced

1 14.5-oz. can beef broth

1 14.5-oz. can diced tomatoes,
   undrained

1½ cups water

1 tsp. unsweetened cocoa
   powder

4 cups dried wide noodles
   (6 oz.)

1½ cups thinly sliced cabbage

2 tsp. paprika

¼ cup light sour cream
   Snipped fresh parsley
   (optional)

1. Sprinkle meat with salt and pepper. Cut meat into ½-inch cubes. In a 3- to 4-qt. pot heat oil over medium-high heat. Add meat; cook and stir about 6 minutes or until browned. Add carrots, onion, and garlic; cook and stir 3 minutes more or until onion softens.

2. Stir in the the next four ingredients (through cocoa powder). Bring to boiling; reduce heat. Simmer, uncovered, 10 minutes.

3. Stir in the uncooked noodles, cabbage, and paprika. Simmer, uncovered, 5 to 7 minutes more or until noodles are tender but still firm, stirring occasionally. Remove from heat. Top servings with sour cream and, if desired, parsley and additional paprika.

PER SERVING: *321 cal., 7 g fat (2 g sat. fat), 74 mg chol., 694 mg sodium, 43 g carb., 5 g fiber, 7 g sugars, 22 g pro.*

southwestern noodle bowl

START TO FINISH: 30 minutes | **MAKES:** 6 to 8 servings (1⅓ cups each)

1½ lb. beef flank steak or beef top round steak, trimmed of fat

½ tsp. ground cumin

¼ tsp. salt

⅛ tsp. black pepper

2 Tbsp. vegetable oil

2 cloves garlic, minced

1 32-oz. box reduced-sodium beef broth

5 oz. dried angel hair pasta, broken

1½ cups chopped red and/or yellow sweet peppers or frozen mixed vegetables

6 green onions, cut into 1-inch pieces

½ cup hot-style salsa

1. Cut meat into thin bite-size strips. Sprinkle meat with cumin, salt, and black pepper.

2. In a 4- to 5-qt. pot heat 1 Tbsp. of the oil over medium-high heat. Add garlic; cook and stir 15 seconds. Add half of the meat; cook and stir 2 minutes or until slightly pink in center. Remove meat from pan. Repeat with the remaining 1 Tbsp. oil and the remaining meat. Set meat aside.

3. Add broth to the hot pot; bring to boiling. Stir in the remaining ingredients; return to boiling. Cook, uncovered, about 5 minutes or until pasta is tender, stirring occasionally. Remove pot from heat. Return meat to the pot; cover and let stand until heated through.

PER SERVING: *322 cal., 11 g fat (3 g sat. fat), 70 mg chol., 569 mg sodium, 23 g carb., 2 g fiber, 4 g sugars, 30 g pro.*

SIMPLE SWAP

Prefer chicken to beef? You can substitute skinless, boneless chicken breast for the steak. In Step 2, cook the chicken until it is no longer pink and use chicken broth in place of the beef broth.

swedish meatball pasta pot

PREP: 10 minutes | **COOK:** 45 minutes | **MAKES:** 6 servings (1 cup each)

- 1 32-oz. box reduced-sodium beef broth
- 1 Tbsp. Worcestershire sauce
- ¼ tsp. ground nutmeg
- ¼ tsp. ground allspice
- 1 14-oz. pkg. frozen meatballs, thawed
- 3 Tbsp. all-purpose flour
- 3 Tbsp. butter, softened
- 2 cups dried mini farfalle or mini penne pasta (8 oz.)
- ½ cup water
- ½ cup sour cream
  Black pepper
- 1 Tbsp. snipped fresh dill weed (optional)

1. In a 3- to 4-qt. nonstick pot stir together the first four ingredients (through allspice). Add meatballs. Bring to a gentle boil over medium-high heat; reduce heat. Cook, covered, 30 minutes, stirring occasionally.

2. In a small bowl stir together flour and butter to make a paste; stir into the broth mixture. Add pasta and the water; increase heat to medium. Simmer, covered, about 15 minutes or until pasta is tender, stirring occasionally. Remove pot from heat. Stir in sour cream. Season to taste with pepper. If desired, sprinkle with dill weed.

PER SERVING: 445 cal., 27 g fat (12 g sat. fat), 48 mg chol., 853 mg sodium, 38 g carb., 3 g fiber, 4 g sugars, 15 g pro.

beefy chili mac pictured on *page 56*

PREP: 30 minutes | **COOK:** 25 minutes | **MAKES:** 6 servings (1½ cups each)

1½ lb. ground beef

1 cup chopped onion

¾ cup chopped green sweet pepper

3 cloves garlic, minced

2½ cups reduced-sodium beef broth

1 15-oz. can chili beans in chili gravy, undrained

1 14.5-oz. can diced tomatoes and green chiles, undrained

1 8-oz. can no-salt-added tomato sauce

2 tsp. chili powder

1 tsp. ground cumin

¼ tsp. salt

8 oz. dried cavatappi pasta or macaroni

Shredded cheddar cheese and/or corn chips (optional)

1. In a 5- to 6-qt. pot cook ground beef, onion, sweet pepper, and garlic over medium-high heat 5 minutes or until meat is browned. Drain off fat.

2. Stir the next seven ingredients (through salt) into meat mixture in pot. Bring to boiling; reduce heat. Simmer, covered, 15 minutes. Stir in pasta. Simmer, uncovered, 10 to 12 minutes more or until pasta is tender, stirring occasionally. If desired, serve with cheese and/or corn chips

TO MAKE AHEAD: The night before, cook pasta according to package directions. Drain, rinse, and drain again. Place in a covered container and refrigerate overnight. Cook ground beef, onion, sweet pepper, and garlic as directed in Step 1. Drain off fat. Stir in the next seven ingredients (through salt); cool meat mixture slightly. Pour meat mixture into a large bowl. Cover and refrigerate overnight. To serve, return meat mixture to the pot. Bring to a gentle boil over medium heat, stirring occasionally. Stir in pasta. Cover and cook until heated through, stirring occasionally. Serve as directed.

PER SERVING: *529 cal., 22 g fat (8 g sat. fat), 78 mg chol., 764 mg sodium, 51 g carb., 9 g fiber, 8 g sugars, 31 g pro.*

TRY TURKEY

Lighten up this kid-favorite dish by using ground turkey in place of the ground beef and using chicken broth instead of the beef broth.

pasta fagioli

PREP: 20 minutes | **COOK:** 20 minutes | **MAKES:** 8 servings (1½ cups each)

1 32-oz. box reduced-sodium chicken broth

2 15-oz. cans cannellini beans (white kidney beans), rinsed and drained

1 28-oz. can crushed tomatoes with Italian seasoning*

1¼ cups dried ditalini pasta

¾ cup dry red wine or water

½ cup finely chopped onion

1 2.8- to 3-oz. pkg. cooked bacon pieces

3 cloves garlic, thinly sliced

1 tsp. salt

¼ tsp. crushed red pepper
Fresh oregano (optional)

2 Tbsp. balsamic vinegar

1. In a 4- to 5-qt. pot combine the first 10 ingredients (through crushed red pepper). Bring to boiling; reduce heat. Simmer, covered, 12 minutes or until pasta is tender. If desired, top with fresh oregano. Serve with balsamic vinegar.

*TIP: If you can't find canned crushed tomatoes with Italian seasoning, use regular canned crushed tomatoes and add ½ tsp. dried Italian seasoning, crushed.

PER SERVING: 269 cal., 4 g fat (1 g sat. fat), 10 mg chol., 1,215 mg sodium, 38 g carb., 6 g fiber, 5 g sugars, 14 g pro.

PASTA SUB

Ditalini is a short, tubular pasta. If you can't find this shape, any medium-size pasta will do.

classic osso buco

PREP: 35 minutes | **COOK:** 2 hours | **MAKES:** 6 servings

1 Tbsp. olive oil

1 lb. beef or veal shank crosscuts, cut 1 to 2 inches thick

8 oz. beef or veal stew meat, cut into 1-inch pieces

1 cup chopped onion

½ cup finely chopped carrot

6 cloves garlic, minced

2 Tbsp. all-purpose flour

1 28-oz. can whole tomatoes, undrained

½ cup dry white wine

½ cup chicken broth

1½ tsp. salt

½ tsp. freshly ground black pepper

¼ tsp. dried thyme, crushed

Hot cooked pappardelle pasta or other pasta

Grated Parmesan cheese (optional)

1. In a 4- to 5-qt. pot heat oil over medium-high heat. Add shanks and stew meat; cook 5 minutes or until well browned on all sides. Using a slotted spoon, remove meat.

2. Add onion and carrot to pot; cook over medium heat 5 minutes, stirring occasionally. Add garlic; cook and stir 30 seconds. Sprinkle with flour; cook and stir 1 minute more. Carefully add the next six ingredients (through thyme), stirring to break up tomatoes. Return meat to pot. Bring to boiling; reduce heat. Simmer, covered, 2 hours or until meat is very tender.

3. Remove shanks; cool slightly. Separate meat and marrow from bones; discard bones. Return meat and marrow to pot. Serve with pasta and, if desired, top with cheese.

PER SERVING: *490 cal., 7 g fat (2 g sat. fat), 80 mg chol., 932 mg sodium, 68 g carb., 6 g fiber, 7 g sugars, 34 g pro.*

IN A NAME

In Italian, "osso buco" means "bone with a hole," which refers to the shank cut of meat used to make the classic dish. If your grocery story doesn't carry this cut, you can ask the butcher to order it for you.

sausage-eggplant baked ziti

PREP: 25 minutes | **SLOW COOK:** 6 to 7 hours (low) or 3 to 3½ hours (high) + 40 minutes (high)
stand: 5 minutes | **MAKES:** 6 servings (1¼ cups each)

4 oz. bulk sweet Italian sausage

4 cups chopped, peeled eggplant

2 medium bulbs fennel, trimmed, cored, and thinly sliced

1 14.5-oz. can crushed fire-roasted tomatoes, undrained

½ cup water

¼ cup dry white wine

2 Tbsp. tomato paste

2 cloves garlic, minced

1 tsp. dried Italian seasoning, crushed

6 to 8 oz. dried cut ziti or penne pasta

½ cup snipped fresh basil

1 cup shredded part-skim mozzarella cheese (4 oz.)

1. In a large skillet cook sausage over medium-high heat until browned. Drain off fat.*

2. In a 5- to 6-qt. slow cooker combine sausage and the next eight ingredients (through Italian seasoning). Cover and cook on low 6 to 7 hours or on high 3 to 3½ hours.

3. If using low, turn cooker to high. Stir in pasta and basil; cover and cook 30 minutes. Stir pasta mixture; sprinkle with cheese. Cover and cook 10 minutes more. Let stand, uncovered, 5 to 10 minutes before serving. If desired, sprinkle with additional basil.

*TIP: To make this dish quicker, omit Step 1. Combine the first nine ingredients (through Italian seasoning) in the slow cooker. Use a wooden spoon to break raw sausage apart into small pieces. Continue as directed.

PER SERVING: *255 cal., 5 g fat (3 g sat. fat), 18 mg chol., 479 mg sodium, 38 g carb., 6 g fiber, 7 g sugars, 14 g pro.*

ALL ABOUT EGGPLANT

When purchasing eggplant, look for one with firm, glossy skin that is heavy for its size. It should be free from bruising or brown spots.

creamy chicken alfredo

PREP: 15 minutes | **COOK:** 16 minutes | **MAKES:** 8 servings (1 cup each)

1 32-oz. box reduced-sodium chicken broth

1 cup water

1 Tbsp. minced garlic

¼ tsp. black pepper

2 6-oz. pkg. refrigerated grilled chicken strips, cut up (about 2 cups) (tip, *right*)

12 oz. dried rigatoni pasta

1 cup heavy cream

2 Tbsp. all-purpose flour

1 2.8- to 3-oz. pkg. cooked bacon pieces

1 cup frozen peas

1 cup grated Parmesan cheese

1. In a 4- to 5-qt. pot combine the first four ingredients (through pepper). Bring to boiling over high heat. Stir in chicken and pasta; reduce heat. Simmer, covered, 8 minutes.

2. Meanwhile, whisk together heavy cream and flour. If desired, set aside 1 Tbsp. of the bacon for serving. Stir the remaining bacon, the cream mixture, peas, and Parmesan cheese into chicken mixture in pot. Return to a gentle boil over medium-high heat; reduce heat to medium-low. Cook, covered, about 8 minutes or until sauce is thickened and pasta is tender. Sprinkle with reserved bacon (if using).

TO MAKE AHEAD: Use a slow cooker with a removable liner. Combine the first five ingredients (through chicken) in the liner. Cover and refrigerate overnight. The next day, let the liner stand at room temperature 15 minutes. Place liner in the cooker unit; stir in pasta. Cover and cook on high 2 hours. Whisk together heavy cream and flour. Stir cream mixture, bacon, peas, and Parmesan into chicken mixture in cooker. Cover and cook on high 15 minutes.

PER SERVING: *424 cal., 17 g fat (10 g sat. fat), 82 mg chol., 1,015 mg sodium, 39 g carb., 2 g fiber, 3 g sugars, 27 g pro.*

CHICKEN CHOICES

If you prefer, you can use 12 ounces leftover cooked chicken, deli-roasted chicken, or frozen grilled chicken strips (thawed). Or poach your own chicken to use in the recipe: Cook 1 pound skinless, boneless chicken breasts in simmering water in a covered large skillet for 15 to 20 minutes or until cooked through (165°F). Cool slightly then chop or shred into pieces.

| FAST PREP

thai chicken noodles

START TO FINISH: 35 minutes | **MAKES:** 6 servings (1 cup each)

1 cup canned crushed tomatoes*

½ cup chunky peanut butter

1 Tbsp. vegetable oil

1 lb. skinless, boneless chicken thighs or breasts, cut into 1-inch pieces

1 Tbsp. minced garlic

2 tsp. grated fresh ginger or ½ tsp. ground ginger

2 14.5-oz. cans reduced-sodium chicken broth

1 serrano or jalapeño chile pepper, seeded and finely chopped (tip, *page 14*) (optional)

1 Tbsp. fish sauce (optional)

4 oz. dried rice noodles, broken if desired

2 cups shredded green cabbage

¼ cup chopped green onions

Snipped fresh cilantro (optional)

Coarsely chopped peanuts (optional)

1. In a small bowl whisk together tomatoes and peanut butter; set aside. In a 4- to 5-qt. pot heat oil over medium-high heat. Add chicken, garlic, and ginger; cook about 7 minutes or until chicken is browned, stirring occasionally.

2. Add tomato mixture and broth to chicken in pot. If desired, stir in chile pepper and fish sauce. Bring to boiling. Stir in noodles and cabbage; reduce heat. Simmer, uncovered, 5 minutes or until noodles and cabbage are tender, stirring occasionally. Remove pot from heat. Stir in green onions. If desired, top servings with cilantro and peanuts.

*TIP: If you can only find crushed tomatoes in a 28-oz. can, you will have some left over. Place the extra tomatoes in an airtight container, cover, and store in the refrigerator up to 3 days or freeze up to 3 months. Use in pasta sauces or soups.

PER SERVING: *338 cal., 16 g fat (3 g sat. fat), 71 mg chol., 614 mg sodium, 25 g carb., 3 g fiber, 5 g sugars, 24 g pro.*

Gnocchi, Sweet Corn, and Arugula in
Cream Sauce, *page 99*

going
meatless

When veggie-centered main dishes are this hearty and filling,
skipping the meat is anyday easy.

stewed favas with fennel and sweet potatoes

START TO FINISH: 35 minutes | MAKES: 8 servings (1⅓ cups each)

¼ cup olive oil

1 cup chopped onion

1 small fennel bulb, trimmed, cored, and chopped (1 cup)

6 cloves garlic, minced

1 tsp. ground cumin

1 tsp. ground coriander

1 tsp. caraway seeds, crushed

¼ tsp. ground turmeric

2 bay leaves

3 19-oz. cans fava beans, rinsed and drained

3 cups reduced-sodium chicken or vegetable broth

2 lb. sweet potatoes, peeled and cut into ¾-inch pieces

1 tsp. salt

¼ cup butter, softened

1 Tbsp. orange zest

1. In a large pot heat oil over medium heat. Add onion and fennel; cook 6 minutes or until tender, stirring occasionally. Add the next six ingredients (through bay leaves); cook 1 minute. Add beans, broth, sweet potatoes, and salt to pot. Bring to boiling; reduce heat. Simmer, covered, 12 to 15 minutes or until sweet potatoes are tender. Discard bay leaves.

2. Stir in butter and orange zest; toss to coat.

PER SERVING: 462 cal., 15 g fat (6 g sat. fat), 21 mg chol., 694 mg sodium, 65 g carb., 19 g fiber, 11 g sugars, 20 g pro.

"RIBOLLITA" DEFINED: THIS FAMOUS TUSCAN-STYLE SOUP, FOR WHICH THERE ARE COUNTLESS VARIATIONS, INCLUDES A HEARTY COMBO OF VEGGIES, LEGUMES, AND CHUNKS OF STALE BREAD THAT THICKEN THE SOUP.

chickpea ribollita

START TO FINISH: 1 hour 10 minutes | **MAKES:** 6 servings (1½ cups each)

2 tsp. olive oil

⅔ cup thinly sliced leeks

4 cloves garlic, minced

2 15-oz. cans garbanzo beans (chickpeas), rinsed and drained

1 28-oz. can no-salt-added whole peeled tomatoes, undrained and cut up

3 cups reduced-sodium chicken broth

1 cup water

1 bay leaf

2 tsp. herbes de Provence

½ tsp. freshly ground black pepper

¼ to ½ tsp. crushed red pepper

8 oz. Brussels sprouts, trimmed and very thinly sliced (3 cups)

½ cup snipped fresh basil and/or parsley

1 recipe Herbed Croutons or 4 cups purchased croutons

3 Tbsp. grated Parmesan cheese

1. In a 4-qt. pot heat oil over medium heat. Add leeks; cook and stir 4 minutes or until softened. Add garlic; cook and stir 1 minute more.

2. Add the next eight ingredients (through crushed red pepper). Bring to boiling, stirring occasionally; reduce heat. Simmer, covered, 30 minutes, adding Brussels sprouts the last 5 minutes.

3. Discard bay leaf. Stir in basil and half of the croutons; let stand 5 minutes. Sprinkle servings with cheese and the remaining croutons.

HERBED CROUTONS: Preheat oven to 350°F. Cut 8 oz. ciabatta bread into 1-inch cubes (5 cups). Spread bread in a 15×10-inch baking pan. Bake 10 minutes. Transfer to a large bowl. Meanwhile, in a blender or small food processor combine ¼ cup olive oil, 3 Tbsp. snipped fresh parsley, 2 Tbsp. each snipped fresh chives and snipped fresh basil, 1 tsp. lemon juice, and 1 clove garlic, minced. Cover and blend or process until smooth. Spoon herb mixture over hot bread cubes; toss to coat. Return to baking pan. Bake 13 to 15 minutes more or until croutons are crisp and edges are golden, stirring once. Makes 4 cups.

PER SERVING: *359 cal., 14 g fat (2 g sat. fat), 4 mg chol., 691 mg sodium, 47 g carb., 9 g fiber, 9 g sugars, 14 g pro.*

spanish-style gigante beans

PREP: 30 minutes | **STAND:** 1 hour | **COOK:** 1 hour | **BAKE:** 45 minutes at 350°F
MAKES: 6 servings (1⅓ cups each)

1 lb. dried gigante or large
  butter beans (lima beans)
  (tip, *right*)

2 Tbsp. olive oil

½ cup finely chopped onion

6 cloves garlic, minced

2 pints grape tomatoes

1 cup bottled roasted red
  sweet peppers, chopped

2 tsp. smoked paprika

¼ tsp. saffron threads, crushed

2 bay leaves

2 tsp. salt

½ cup marcona almonds or
  salted roasted almonds,
  chopped

1 recipe Parsley Topper
  (optional)

1. Rinse beans. In an oven-safe 4-qt. pot combine beans and 8 cups water. Bring to boiling; reduce heat. Simmer, covered, 2 minutes. Remove from heat. Let stand, covered, 1 hour. (Or place beans and water in pot. Cover and let soak in the refrigerator overnight.) Drain beans; rinse and return to pot. Add fresh water to cover beans by 1 inch. Cover and bring to boiling; reduce heat. Simmer, covered, 45 minutes or until beans are tender, stirring occasionally. Drain beans in a colander, reserving 2 cups of the cooking liquid. Set beans and liquid aside.

2. Preheat oven to 350°F. Heat oil in the same pot over medium heat. Add onion and garlic; cook 3 to 4 minutes or until tender. Add the next five ingredients (through bay leaves). Bring to boiling; reduce heat to medium-low. Simmer, uncovered, 15 minutes or until tomatoes start to break down, stirring occasionally. Stir in beans, salt, and the reserved liquid. Bring to boiling. Bake, uncovered, 45 minutes. Discard bay leaves. Top with almonds and, if desired, Parsley Topper.

PER SERVING: 283 cal., 16 g fat (2 g sat. fat), 0 mg chol., 898 mg sodium, 28 g carb., 8 g fiber, 7 g sugars, 10 g pro.

PARSLEY TOPPER: In a small bowl combine 1 cup finely chopped Italian parsley, 2 Tbsp. olive oil, and 2 cloves garlic, minced. Mash with the back of a spoon.

SKIP A STEP

To speed up prep for this recipe, use canned beans instead of dried ones. Just rinse and drain four 16-ounce cans butter beans and stir in as directed in Step 2. Use 2 cups fresh water instead of the 2 cups bean cooking liquid.

lemony white bean and carrot spinach salad

PREP: 30 minutes | **STAND:** 1 hour | **SLOW COOK:** 7 to 8 hours (low) or 3½ to 4 hours (high)
MAKES: 6 servings (1½ cups each)

- 1½ cups dried Great Northern beans
- 5 medium carrots, cut into ½-inch pieces
- 1 medium onion, halved and thinly sliced
- 2 cloves garlic, minced
- ½ tsp. dried oregano, crushed
- ¼ tsp. salt
- ¼ tsp. black pepper
- 4½ cups reduced-sodium chicken stock
- 1 lemon
- 1 5-oz. pkg. fresh baby spinach
- 1 medium avocado, halved, seeded, peeled, and sliced

  Lemon slices (optional)
- ¾ cup crumbled reduced-fat feta cheese (3 oz.)
- ⅓ cup pistachio nuts, coarsely chopped

1. Rinse beans; drain. In a 4- to 5-qt. pot combine beans and enough water to cover beans by 2 inches. Bring to boiling; reduce heat. Simmer, uncovered, 10 minutes. Remove from heat. Cover and let stand 1 hour. Rinse and drain beans.

2. In a 3½- or 4-qt. slow cooker combine the soaked beans and the next six ingredients (through pepper). Add chicken stock. Cover and cook on low 7 to 8 hours or on high 3½ to 4 hours.

3. Remove 2 tsp. zest and squeeze 3 Tbsp. juice from the lemon. If desired, remove ½ cup of the cooking liquid from cooker; set aside. Drain bean mixture; discard any remaining cooking liquid. Return bean mixture to the hot cooker. Stir in lemon zest and juice.

4. Line a platter with spinach; top with bean mixture. If desired, drizzle with enough of the reserved cooking liquid to moisten. Serve with avocado and, if desired, lemon slices. Top with cheese and pistachios.

PER SERVING: *319 cal., 9 g fat (2 g sat. fat), 4 mg chol., 498 mg sodium, 43 g carb., 14 g fiber, 5 g sugars, 19 g pro.*

double bean, bulgur, and beer chili

PREP: 20 minutes | **COOK:** 20 minutes | **MAKES:** 8 servings (1⅓ cups each)

1 28-oz. can crushed tomatoes

2 cups water

2 15-oz. cans red kidney beans, rinsed and drained

1 15-oz. can black-eyed peas, rinsed and drained

1 12-oz. bottle light wheat beer

1 cup chopped onion

1 cup chopped green sweet pepper

1 cup chopped red sweet pepper

1 cup uncooked bulgur

4 large cloves garlic, minced

2 Tbsp. packed brown sugar

1 Tbsp. chili powder

1½ tsp. ground cumin

1 tsp. dried oregano, crushed

1 tsp. salt

Toppings such as shredded cheddar cheese, sour cream, chopped red onion, sliced green onions, roasted pumpkin seeds, and/or chili powder (optional)

1. In a 5- to 6-qt. pot combine the first 15 ingredients (through salt). Bring to boiling; reduce heat. Simmer, covered, 20 minutes or until bulgur is tender. Serve with desired toppings.

TIP: If desired, for fuller flavor, cook and stir the onion, peppers, and garlic in 1 Tbsp. hot vegetable oil until softened and fragrant before adding other ingredients.

TO MAKE AHEAD: Cover and refrigerate chili up to 3 days. (Or place chili in a freezer container, label, and freeze up to 3 months. Thaw overnight in the refrigerator before serving.) Heat through before serving, adding a little water, if necessary, for desired consistency.

PER SERVING: 249 cal., 2 g fat (0 g sat. fat), 0 mg chol., 769 mg sodium, 49 g carb., 11 g fiber, 11 g sugars, 12 g pro.

| FAST PREP | MAKE AHEAD

refried beans

PREP: 20 minutes | **STAND:** 1 hour | **COOK:** 2 hours 30 minutes | **MAKES:** 4 servings (½ cup each)

8 oz. dried pinto beans (about 1¼ cups)

1 tsp. salt

2 Tbsp. olive oil

½ cup chopped onion

1 Tbsp. minced garlic

Black pepper

1. Rinse beans. In a 3-qt. pot combine beans and 4 cups water. Bring to boiling; reduce heat. Simmer, covered, 2 minutes. Remove from heat. Cover and let stand 1 hour. (Or place beans and water in pan. Cover and let soak in a cool place overnight.) Drain and rinse beans.

2. In the same pot combine beans, 4 cups fresh water, and the salt. Bring to boiling; reduce heat. Simmer, covered, 2½ to 3 hours or until beans are very tender. Drain beans in a colander, reserving liquid.

3. Rinse and dry pot. In the same pot heat oil over medium heat. Add onion and garlic; cook until tender. Add beans; mash thoroughly with a potato masher. Stir in enough of the cooking liquid (about ¼ to ½ cup) until mixture reaches a pastelike consistency. Cook, uncovered, over low heat 8 to 10 minutes or until thick, stirring often. Season to taste with additional salt and pepper.

TIP: If you like, add one 4-oz. can diced green chiles or ¼ cup chopped pickled jalapeños, 1 tsp. chili powder, and/or 1 tsp. ground cumin. You also may substitute 4 cups vegetable broth for the water in Step 2.

TO MAKE AHEAD: Prepare beans through Step 2. Place beans and cooking liquid in separate containers; cover and store in refrigerator up to 24 hours. To serve, continue as directed in Step 3.

PER SERVING: 268 cal., 7 g fat (1 g sat. fat), 0 mg chol., 597 mg sodium, 38 g carb., 9 g fiber, 2 g sugars, 13 g pro.

USE IT UP

Protein-rich refried beans provide an easy substitute for meat in Mexican dishes. Use them to make tostadas, quesadillas, burritos, nachos, enchiladas, and Mexican seven-layer dip.

red beans creole

PREP: 10 minutes | **COOK:** 20 minutes | **STAND:** 10 minutes | **MAKES:** 5 servings (1 cup each)

1 15-oz. can red beans or red kidney beans, rinsed and drained (tip, *opposite*)

1 14.5-oz. can no-salt-added diced tomatoes with basil, garlic, and oregano, undrained

1 14.4-oz. pkg. frozen pepper stir-fry vegetables (green, red, and yellow sweet peppers and onions)

1 cup uncooked converted rice

1 cup water

1 Tbsp. Creole seasoning

1 Tbsp. minced garlic

Bottled hot pepper sauce (optional)

1. In a 3- to 4-qt. pot combine the first seven ingredients (through garlic). Bring to boiling over medium-high heat, stirring to break up vegetables. Reduce heat. Simmer, covered, 20 minutes or until rice is tender and most of the liquid is absorbed. Remove from heat. Let stand 10 minutes before serving. If desired, serve with hot pepper sauce.

PER SERVING: *260 cal., 0 g fat, 0 mg chol., 1,173 mg sodium, 54 g carb., 11 g fiber, 10 g sugars, 9 g pro.*

TO CUT THE SODIUM, OPT FOR REDUCED-SODIUM OR NO-SALT-ADDED RED KIDNEY BEANS IN PLACE OF THE RED BEANS IN THIS RECIPE.

bbq veggie joes

PREP: 15 minutes | **COOK:** 45 minutes | **MAKES:** 16 servings (1 sandwich each)

- 2 14.5-oz. cans vegetable or chicken broth
- 8 oz. portobello or cremini mushrooms, chopped (3 cups)
- 1 15-oz. can tomato sauce
- 1 cup chopped carrots
- ⅔ cup dried lentils, rinsed and drained
- ⅔ cup uncooked regular brown rice
- ½ cup chopped onion
- 3 Tbsp. cider vinegar
- 2 Tbsp. packed brown sugar
- 2 Tbsp. yellow mustard
- ½ tsp. salt
- 1 clove garlic, minced
- ¼ to ½ tsp. cayenne pepper
- 16 whole wheat hamburger buns or French-style rolls, split and toasted

  Toppings such as chopped red onion, sliced pickles, chopped tomato, and/or coarsely shredded iceberg lettuce

1. In a 3- to 4-qt. pot combine the first 13 ingredients (through cayenne pepper). Bring to boiling; reduce heat. Simmer, covered, 45 to 50 minutes or until lentils and rice are tender, stirring occasionally.

2. Use a slotted spoon to spoon remaining mixture onto buns. Add desired toppings.

TO MAKE AHEAD: Place mixture in a storage container. Cover and chill up to 3 days or freeze up to 3 months. To serve, thaw in refrigerator overnight, if frozen. Transfer mixture to a medium saucepan; cover and bring to simmering over low heat, stirring ocassionally. If necessary, add water to make desired consistency.

PER SERVING: 313 cal., 3 g fat (1 g sat. fat), 0 mg chol., 863 mg sodium, 60 g carb., 4 g fiber, 7 g sugars, 11 g pro.

indian-spiced lentils with spinach

PREP: 15 minutes | **SLOW COOK:** 8 hours (low) or 4 hours (high) | **MAKES:** 8 servings (1⅓ cups each)

5 cups reduced-sodium chicken or vegetable broth

3 cups dried brown lentils, rinsed and drained

1 14.5-oz. can diced tomatoes, undrained

1 cup finely chopped carrots

½ cup chopped onion

2 fresh serrano chile peppers, halved, seeded, and finely chopped (tip, *page 14*)

1 tsp. salt

1 tsp. ground cumin

1 tsp. ground coriander

½ tsp. ground turmeric

1 14-oz. can unsweetened coconut milk

1 5-oz. pkg. fresh baby spinach

Salt and black pepper

Hot cooked basmati rice or brown rice

Orange wedges

1. In a 5- to 6-qt. slow cooker combine the first 10 ingredients (through turmeric).

2. Cover and cook on low 8 hours or on high 4 hours. Stir in coconut milk and spinach. Season to taste with salt and black pepper. If desired, serve with hot cooked rice and orange wedges.

PER SERVING: 496 cal., 9 g fat (8 g sat. fat), 0 mg chol., 823 mg sodium, 81 g carb., 10 g fiber, 7 g sugars, 23 g pro.

veggie-stuffed peppers

PREP: 30 minutes | **SLOW COOK:** 3 hours (low) | **MAKES:** 4 servings (1 stuffed pepper each)

4 medium red, orange, and/or yellow sweet peppers

2 cups cooked brown or white rice

2 cups coarsely chopped kale or Swiss chard

2 medium tomatoes, chopped

½ cup crumbled feta cheese (2 oz.)

¼ cup thinly sliced green onions

2 tsp. dried Italian seasoning, crushed

½ tsp. salt

¼ tsp. black pepper

¼ cup water

¼ cup coarsely chopped fresh Italian parsley

¼ cup chopped pitted Kalamata olives

¼ cup crumbled feta cheese (1 oz.) (optional)

1 Tbsp. lemon zest

1 tsp. olive oil

2 Tbsp. chopped walnuts, toasted (tip, *page 31*) (optional)

1. Cut off tops of peppers and, if desired, set aside for serving. Trim bottoms of peppers so they sit upright. Remove and discard seeds and membranes. In a large bowl combine the next eight ingredients (through black pepper). Pour the ¼ cup water into a 3½- to 6-qt. oval slow cooker. Place peppers in slow cooker (open sides up). Spoon rice mixture into peppers. Add pepper tops if using. Cover and cook on low about 3 hours or until peppers are tender.

2. Carefully transfer peppers to a platter; discard cooking liquid. In a small bowl stir together the next five ingredients (through olive oil). Spoon olive mixture over peppers. If desired, sprinkle with walnuts.

PER SERVING: *271 cal., 10 g fat (3 g sat. fat), 17 mg chol., 585 mg sodium, 37 g carb., 7 g fiber, 8 g sugars, 9 g pro.*

gnocchi, sweet corn, and arugula in cream sauce

START TO FINISH: 25 minutes | **MAKES:** 4 servings (1 cup each)

1 lb. shelf-stable potato gnocchi

2 cups frozen whole kernel corn

¾ cup half-and-half

3 oz. cream cheese, cut up

½ tsp. garlic powder

½ tsp. dried basil or oregano, crushed

½ tsp. salt

¼ tsp. freshly ground black pepper

3 cups torn fresh arugula

Crushed red pepper (optional)

1. In a 4- to 5-qt. pot cook gnocchi and corn according to gnocchi package directions. Drain gnocchi and corn in a colander, reserving ½ cup of the pasta water.

2. For sauce, in the same pot combine the next six ingredients (through black pepper). Cook and stir over medium heat until cream cheese melts and sauce is smooth. Stir in reserved pasta water.

3. Stir cooked gnocchi and corn into sauce in the pot; heat through. Stir in arugula. If desired, sprinkle with crushed red pepper.

PER SERVING: 406 cal., 14 g fat (8 g sat. fat), 37 mg chol., 789 mg sodium, 64 g carb., 5 g fiber, 5 g sugars, 10 g pro.

Mexican Fondue, *page 117*

extra cheese, please

Toss it with pasta, layer it in sandwiches, turn it into dip—what can't you do with cheese? Each of these simple but scrumptious recipes showcases cheese in all its melty, creamy, delectable glory.

stovetop ravioli lasagna

START TO FINISH: 25 minutes | **MAKES:** 4 servings (1½ cups each)

1   egg, lightly beaten

½   of a 15-oz. carton fat-free ricotta cheese

2   Tbsp. grated Romano or Parmesan cheese

2   cups low-sodium tomato pasta sauce with basil

¾   cup water

2   8- to 9-oz. pkg. refrigerated ravioli or agnolotti

2   cups chopped fresh kale

     Crushed red pepper (optional)

1. In a medium bowl combine egg, ricotta cheese, and Romano cheese.

2. In a 3-qt. pot combine pasta sauce and the water. Bring to boiling. Stir in ravioli and kale. Return to boiling; reduce heat. Spoon ricotta mixture into large mounds on top of ravioli mixture.

3. Simmer, covered, about 10 minutes or until ricotta mixture is set and ravioli is tender but still firm. If desired, sprinkle with crushed red pepper.

PER SERVING: 416 cal., 16 g fat (7 g sat. fat), 118 mg chol., 975 mg sodium, 45 g carb., 4 g fiber, 9 g sugars, 26 g pro.

barbecue chicken and bacon macaroni and cheese

PREP: 20 minutes | **SLOW COOK:** 6 hours (low) or 3 hours (high) + 20 minutes (high) | **STAND:** 5 minutes
MAKES: 9 servings (1 cup each)

1   lb. skinless, boneless chicken thighs, cut into 1-inch pieces

2½ cups water

½   cup chopped onion

½   cup chopped dill pickles

1   Tbsp. yellow mustard

12 slices lower-sodium bacon, crisp-cooked and crumbled

1   12-oz. pkg. no-boil, no-drain rotini pasta, such as Barilla Pronto

8   oz. sliced American cheese, torn into bite-size pieces

¼   to ½ cup whole milk

¾   cup bottled barbecue sauce

⅓   cup finely chopped red onion

1. In a 4-qt. slow cooker combine the first five ingredients (through mustard) and half of the bacon. Cover and cook on low 6 hours or on high 3 hours.

2. If using low, turn cooker to high. Stir in pasta. Cover and cook 10 minutes; stir. Cover and cook 10 minutes more; stir again. Top with the cheese (do not stir). Cover and let stand 5 minutes. Add milk and stir to combine.

3. To serve, drizzle each serving with barbecue sauce and top with remaining bacon and chopped red onion.

TO MAKE AHEAD: If your slow cooker has a warm setting, you can hold the macaroni and cheese up to 2 hours. If mixture begins to look dry, stir in up to ½ cup additional milk to reach desired consistency.

PER SERVING: 388 cal., 16 g fat (8 g sat. fat), 84 mg chol., 904 mg sodium, 40 g carb., 0 g fiber, 10 g sugars, 22 g pro.

buffalo-ranch macaroni and cheese

PREP: 15 minutes | **SLOW COOK:** 2 hours 5 minutes (high) | **MAKES:** 8 to 10 servings (1 cup each)

1 14.5-oz. pkg. dried multigrain rotini or penne pasta

1 cup purchased shredded carrot and/or thinly sliced celery

½ to 1 cup bottled cayenne pepper sauce

1 1-oz. envelope ranch dry salad dressing mix

4 cups water

8 oz. sliced American cheese (about 10 to 11 slices), torn into bite-size pieces

Milk (optional)

1. In a 3½- or 4-qt. slow cooker combine the first four ingredients (through dressing mix). Add the water; stir to combine.

2. Cover and cook on high 2 hours (pasta should absorb all the liquid). Add cheese (do not stir). Cover and cook 5 minutes. Stir gently to combine. If desired, add milk to reach desired creaminess.

PER SERVING: *407 cal., 14 g fat (6 g sat. fat), 75 mg chol., 1,382 mg sodium, 39 g carb., 4 g fiber, 3 g sugars, 29 g pro.*

PROTEIN UP

Increase the protein content of this dish by adding some leftover cooked chicken or rotisserie chicken from your supermarket. Prepare as directed, except stir in 3 cups chopped cooked chicken with the cheese in Step 2.

tex-mex cheeseburger shells

START TO FINISH: 25 minutes | **MAKES:** 10 to 12 servings (1 cup each)

2 lb. lean ground beef

1 cup chopped onion

3 cups dried shell macaroni or elbow macaroni (12 oz.)

3 cups shredded Mexican four-cheese blend (12 oz.)

3 cups water

1 16-oz. jar salsa

1 15-oz. jar processed cheese dip

1 4-oz. can diced green chile peppers, undrained

1 2.25-oz. can sliced pitted ripe olives, drained

1 Tbsp. chili powder

½ tsp. ground cumin

Chopped tomato and/or sliced green onions

1. In a 6- to 8-qt. nonstick pot cook ground beef and onion over medium heat until meat is browned. Drain off fat. Stir in the next nine ingredients (through cumin). Bring to boiling over medium-high heat. Reduce heat; cook, uncovered, 12 to 15 minutes or until pasta is tender, stirring frequently. Remove from heat; let stand 5 minutes. Top servings with tomato and/or green onions.

TO MAKE AHEAD: The night before, cook pasta according to package directions. Drain, rinse, and drain again. Place in a covered container and refrigerate overnight. Use a slow cooker with a removable liner. In a large skillet cook ground beef and onion over medium heat until meat is browned. Drain off fat; cool meat mixture slightly. Place meat mixture in the slow cooker liner. Stir in cheese, salsa, cheese dip, chiles, olives, chili powder, and cumin (omit water). Cover and refrigerate overnight. The next day, let the liner stand at room temperature 15 minutes. Place liner in the slow cooker. Cover and cook on low 4 to 5 hours or on high 2 to 2½ hours. Stir cooked macaroni into meat mixture; let stand 15 minutes before serving. Serve as directed.

PER SERVING: 558 cal., 29 g fat (11 g sat. fat), 98 mg chol., 1,033 mg sodium, 39 g carb., 2 g fiber, 7 g sugars, 35 g pro.

peppery italian beef sandwiches

PREP: 30 minutes | ROAST: 2 hours 15 minutes at 325°F | MAKES: 8 servings (1 sandwich each)

1   2½- to 3-lb. boneless beef chuck pot roast, trimmed of fat

1   tsp. garlic-pepper seasoning

1   Tbsp. vegetable oil

1½ cups water

1   16-oz. jar sliced pepperoncini (salad peppers), drained

1   0.5- to 0.75-oz. envelope Italian dry salad dressing mix

2   tsp. dried Italian seasoning, crushed

8   kaiser rolls or hoagie buns, split and toasted

2   cups shredded mozzarella cheese (8 oz.)

1. Preheat oven to 325°F. Sprinkle meat with garlic-pepper seasoning; rub in with your fingers. In an oven-safe 5- to 6-qt. pot heat oil over medium-high heat. Add meat; cook until browned on all sides. Stir in the water, peppers, salad dressing mix, and Italian seasoning. Bring to boiling.

2. Roast, covered, 2¼ to 2½ hours or until meat is tender enough to shred. Transfer meat to a cutting board; shred with two forks. Pour cooking liquid through a strainer, reserving peppers. Skim fat from liquid. Return beef and peppers to pot. Add just enough of the liquid to moisten meat.

3. Spoon shredded meat and peppers into buns; sprinkle with cheese.

TO MAKE AHEAD: Prepare as directed, except do not assemble sandwiches. Place meat, peppers, and liquid in an airtight container. Cover and store in the refrigerator up to 3 days or freeze up to 3 months. To serve, thaw meat mixture overnight in refrigerator, if frozen. Reheat meat mixture in a covered pot over medium heat. Assemble sandwiches as directed in Step 3.

PER SERVING: 522 cal., 25 g fat (10 g sat. fat), 116 mg chol., 1,151 mg sodium, 39 g carb., 2 g fiber, 5 g sugars, 35 g pro.

GO LEANER: CUT THE FAT IN THESE SANDWICHES BY USING A LEANER CUT OF BEEF, SUCH AS BOTTOM ROUND ROAST OR SIRLOIN ROAST.

philly cheese pot roast sandwiches

PREP: 20 minutes | **COOK:** 10 to 12 hours (low) or 5 to 6 hours (high) + 30 minutes (high) | **BROIL:** 1 minute
MAKES: 8 servings (1 sandwich each)

1   2½- to 3-lb. boneless beef chuck pot roast, trimmed of fat

1   cup chopped onion

¼   cup Worcestershire sauce

1   Tbsp. instant beef bouillon granules

2   cloves garlic, minced

1   tsp. dried oregano, crushed

½   tsp. dried basil, crushed

½   tsp. dried thyme, crushed

8   hoagie buns or kaiser rolls, split and toasted

8   slices American cheese, halved diagonally

1. Cut meat into 1-inch pieces. In a 3½- or 4-qt. slow cooker combine meat and the next seven ingredients (through thyme).

2. Cover and cook on low 10 to 12 hours or on high 5 to 6 hours. Stir to break up meat cubes. If using low, turn cooker to high. Cook, uncovered, 30 minutes more, stirring often to break up meat.

3. Use a slotted spoon to place meat mixture in buns. Top with cheese. If desired, sprinkle with additional dried oregano. Place sandwiches on a baking sheet. Broil 4 to 5 inches from the heat about 1 minute or until cheese is melted and bubbly.

TO MAKE AHEAD: Prepare as directed through Step 2. Place meat mixture in an airtight container. Cover and store in the refrigerator up to 3 days or freeze up to 3 months. To serve, thaw meat overnight in refrigerator, if frozen. Reheat meat in a covered pot over medium heat. Assemble sandwiches as directed in Step 3.

PER SERVING: *493 cal., 18 g fat (8 g sat. fat), 122 mg chol., 1,009 mg sodium, 35 g carb., 2 g fiber, 0 g sugars, 46 g pro.*

reuben sandwiches

PREP: 15 minutes | **SLOW COOK:** 12 hours (low) or 6 hours (high) | **MAKES:** 8 servings (1 sandwich each)

1 2- to 3-lb. corned beef brisket with spice packet

1 14- to 16-oz. can or jar sauerkraut, drained

½ cup Thousand Island salad dressing

16 slices rye bread, toasted

8 slices Swiss cheese (about 6 oz.)

Dill pickle slices (optional)

1. Trim fat from corned beef brisket. If necessary, cut meat to fit in a 3½- or 4-qt. slow cooker. Place brisket in cooker. Sprinkle spices from packet evenly over brisket; rub in with your fingers. Add sauerkraut and drizzle the salad dressing over all.

2. Cover and cook on low 12 hours or on high 6 hours.

3. Transfer brisket to a cutting board. Thinly slice brisket against the grain. Return sliced brisket to cooker and stir to combine with cooking liquid.

4. Using a slotted spoon, spoon corned beef mixture onto half of the toasted bread slices and top with cheese. If desired, broil 3 to 4 inches from the heat 1 to 2 minutes or until cheese is melted. If desired, drizzle with additional Thousand Island salad dressing and top with pickle slices. Top with remaining bread.

TO MAKE AHEAD: Prepare corned beef as directed through Step 3 except place meat and liquid in an airtight container. Cover and store in the refrigerator up to 3 days or freeze up to 3 months. To serve, thaw meat overnight in refrigerator, if frozen. Reheat meat in a covered pot over medium heat. Assemble sandwiches as directed in Step 4.

PER SERVING: *508 cal., 27 g fat (9 g sat. fat), 81 mg chol., 1,554 mg sodium, 36 g carb., 5 g fiber, 6 g sugars, 28 g pro.*

vegetable chili con queso

PREP: 20 minutes | **SLOW COOK:** 6 to 7 hours (low) or 3 to 3½ hours (high)
MAKES: 32 servings (¼ cup dip + ½ oz. chips each)

2½ cups chopped zucchini and/or yellow summer squash (tip, *right*)

1 15-oz. can pinto beans, rinsed and drained

1 15-oz. can black beans, rinsed and drained

1 15-oz. can chili beans in chili gravy

1 14.5-oz. can no-salt-added diced tomatoes, undrained

1 cup chopped onion

¼ cup no-salt-added tomato paste

1 fresh jalapeño chile pepper, seeded and finely chopped (tip, *page 14*)

2 to 3 tsp. chili powder

4 cloves garlic, minced

3 cups shredded Colby and Monterey Jack cheese (12 oz.)

16 oz. baked tortilla chips

1. In a 3½- or 4-qt. slow cooker combine the first 10 ingredients (through garlic).

2. Cover and cook on low 6 to 7 hours or on high 3 to 3½ hours. Gradually stir in 2 cups of the cheese until melted. Top with the remaining 1 cup cheese; cover and let stand until melted.* Serve immediately or cover and keep warm on low or warm up to 1 hour. Serve with chips.

*TIP: Or remove dip to a serving bowl and arrange chips around the edge. Top with the 1 cup cheese and let stand until melted. Serve immediately.

PER SERVING: 138 cal., 4 g fat (2 g sat. fat), 9 mg chol., 291 mg sodium, 20 g carb., 4 g fiber, 1 g sugars, 7 g pro.

PERFECT PICKING

Zucchini and yellow summer squash are the main veggies in this queso dip, so be sure to choose quality ones. They should be firm, heavy, and crisp with glossy, brightly colored skin and no bruises or cuts. The stems should appear fresh with no shriveling or discoloration. Generally, the smaller the squash, the better its flavor and texture.

mexican fondue *pictured on page 100*

PREP: 20 minutes | **COOK:** 20 minutes | **MAKES:** 20 servings (¼ cup fondue each)

1 14.5-oz. can diced tomatoes, undrained

1 cup finely chopped cooked chicken

⅔ cup finely chopped onion

1 4-oz. can diced green chile peppers, undrained

12 oz. Monterey Jack cheese with jalapeño peppers or plain Monterey Jack cheese, cubed

1 12-oz. pkg. American cheese slices, torn

Chili powder (optional)

Assorted dippers such as vegetables, cubed corn bread (tip, *right*), toasted flour tortilla wedges, or tortilla chips

Milk (optional)

1. In a 3-qt. pot combine the first four ingredients (through chiles). Add both cheeses; stir gently to combine.

2. Cover and cook over medium-low heat about 20 minutes or until cheese is melted, stirring occasionally.

3. If desired, sprinkle fondue with chili powder. Serve fondue with dippers, swirling pieces as you dip. If the fondue thickens, stir in a little milk. If necessary, keep fondue warm over low heat, covered, up to 1 hour, stirring occasionally.

TO MAKE AHEAD: Transfer fondue to an airtight container. Cover and chill up to 3 days. Reheat in the pot over medium-low heat 15 to 18 minutes, stirring occasionally. Add milk to reach desired consistency.

PER SERVING: *150 cal., 11 g fat (6 g sat. fat), 38 mg chol., 468 mg sodium, 3 g carb., 0 g fiber, 1 g sugars, 9 g pro.*

QUICK CORN BREAD

For an easy dipper, purchase corn bread from your supermarket's bakery or whip one up using a packaged corn bread mix.

mashed potatoes with gouda

START TO FINISH: 40 minutes | **MAKES:** 8 to 10 servings (⅔ cup each)

2   green onions

5   oz. pancetta, cut into ¼-inch cubes (about 1 cup)

1   lb. red-skin potatoes, cut into 1½-inch pieces

1   lb. russet potatoes, peeled and cut into 1½-inch pieces

¾   cup half-and-half or heavy cream

2   cups finely shredded Gouda cheese (8 oz.)

   Salt

   Freshly ground black pepper

1. Thinly slice white portions of green onions. Bias-slice green onion tops and set aside for serving. In a 4-qt. pot cook white portions of onions and the pancetta over medium-high heat about 8 minutes or until pancetta is crisp, stirring occasionally. Remove pancetta mixture. Drain off fat.

2. In the same pot cook potatoes, covered, in enough lightly salted boiling water to cover 20 to 25 minutes or until tender; drain. Return potatoes to pot.

3. Add half-and-half to cooked potatoes. Mash with a potato masher or a mixer on low until nearly smooth. Stir in 1½ cups of the cheese and the pancetta mixture. Season to taste with salt and pepper.

4. Transfer mashed potatoes to a serving dish. Sprinkle with the remaining ½ cup cheese, the green onion tops, and, if desired, additional crisp-cooked pancetta.

TO MAKE AHEAD: Prepare as directed through Step 3. Transfer mashed potatoes to a greased 2-qt. baking dish. Cover and chill up to 24 hours. Preheat oven to 350°F. Bake, covered with foil, 40 to 45 minutes or until heated through.

PER SERVING: *272 cal., 16 g fat (9 g sat. fat), 47 mg chol., 502 mg sodium, 21 g carb., 2 g fiber, 2 g sugars, 13 g pro.*

FAST PREP

ancho butternut
squash gratin

PREP: 25 minutes | **BAKE:** 1 hour at 350°F | **STAND:** 15 minutes | **MAKES:** 8 servings (⅔ cup each)

1 Tbsp. olive oil

6 oz. smoked sausage, bias-sliced

1 cup thinly sliced leeks (3 medium)

1 10.5-oz. can condensed cream of celery soup

1 tsp. ground ancho chile pepper

1 tsp. ground coriander

1 cup shredded Monterey Jack cheese (4 oz.)

1½ lb. butternut squash, peeled, seeded, and sliced ¼ inch thick (5 cups) (tip, *right*)

8 oz. Yukon gold potatoes, peeled and sliced ¼ inch thick (1¼ cups)

Toasted pumpkin seeds (pepitas) and/or snipped fresh cilantro

1. Preheat oven to 350°F. In an oven-safe 4-qt. pot heat oil over medium-high heat. Add sausage and leeks; cook about 7 minutes or until sausage is browned and leeks are tender. Transfer sausage and leeks to a small bowl.

2. In another small bowl combine soup, ancho chile pepper, and coriander. Stir in ¾ cup of the cheese.

3. Cut any large squash slices in half. Layer half of the squash, potatoes, and sausage mixture in the same pot. Top with half of the soup mixture; spread evenly. Repeat layers.

4. Bake, covered, 55 minutes or until vegetables are tender. Uncover; sprinkle with the remaining ¼ cup cheese. Bake 5 minutes more or until cheese is melted. Let stand 15 minutes before serving. Sprinkle servings with pepitas and/or cilantro.

PER SERVING: *224 cal., 14 g fat (5 g sat. fat), 30 mg chol., 465 mg sodium, 17 g carb., 2 g fiber, 3 g sugars, 8 g pro.*

EASY PEELING

To peel a butternut squash, cut off both ends using a large chef's knife. Cut the squash in half lengthwise; scrape out the seeds and fibrous strings from each half. Hold a squash half at an angle on your cutting board and use a sturdy vegetable peeler to peel down its length.

Pork Cassoulet, *page 136*

easy as pot pie

Sure, pot pies in a pot are no surprise,
but these pot pies (plus casseroles)
start and end in the same vessel.
No fuss, no muss for your favorite
comfort food!

burgundy beef stew pot pie

PREP: 35 minutes | **BAKE:** 20 minutes at 375°F | **MAKES:** 6 to 8 servings (1 cup each)

2 to 3 croissants (5 oz. total), split

3 Tbsp. butter, softened

1½ cups coarsely chopped carrots

1½ cups coarsely chopped celery

1 cup frozen small whole onions, thawed and halved

3 cups sliced fresh mushrooms (8 oz.)

1 cup Burgundy (tip, *right*)

1 Tbsp. stone-ground Dijon-style mustard

4 cloves garlic, minced

2 tsp. finely snipped fresh rosemary

2 tsp. dried thyme, crushed

½ tsp. freshly ground black pepper

2 15-oz. pkg. refrigerated cooked beef tips with gravy

1½ cups water

1. Preheat oven to 375°F. Spread cut sides of croissants with 1 Tbsp. of the butter. Cut croissants into 1-inch cubes; set aside.

2. In an oven-safe 5- to 6-qt. pot melt the remaining 2 Tbsp. butter. Add carrots, celery, and onions; cook 5 minutes or until softened. Stir in mushrooms. Cook 7 to 9 minutes or just until vegetables are tender, stirring occasionally. Carefully stir in the next six ingredients (through pepper). Bring to boiling; reduce heat. Simmer, uncovered, 5 minutes or until reduced by half. Stir in beef with gravy and the water; heat through.

3. Sprinkle cubed croissants over beef filling. Bake, uncovered, 20 to 25 minutes or until meat mixture is bubbly and croissants are golden.

TO MAKE AHEAD: Skip Step 1. Prepare beef filling as directed in Step 2. Place filling in an airtight container; cool slightly. Cover and refrigerate up to 3 days. To serve, return filling to pot. Cook, covered, over medium heat until heated through, stirring occasionally. Meanwhile, preheat oven and prepare croissants as directed in Step 1. Sprinkle croissants over hot filling and bake as directed.

PER SERVING: 416 cal., 21 g fat (10 g sat. fat), 92 mg chol., 975 mg sodium, 25 g carb., 3 g fiber, 10 g sugars, 26 g pro.

WINE ABOUT IT

If you don't have Burgundy wine on hand, no worries. Although it is the authentic wine to use for this stew, any dry but fruity red wine, such as Pinot Noir or Shiraz, will do.

vegetable-beef pot pie

PREP: 25 minutes | BAKE: 15 minutes at 400°F | MAKES: 4 to 6 servings (1¼ cups each)

1 lb. lean ground beef or ground turkey

1 cup chopped onion

1 Tbsp. chili powder

½ tsp. kosher salt

⅛ tsp. black pepper

1½ cups frozen peas and carrots or frozen mixed vegetables

1 14.5-oz. can diced tomatoes, undrained

1 13.8-oz. pkg. refrigerated pizza dough

1 egg, lightly beaten (optional)

1. Preheat oven to 400°F. In an oven-safe 3- to 4-qt. pot cook ground meat and onion about 8 minutes or until meat is browned and onion is tender. Drain off fat.

2. Stir chili powder, salt, and pepper into meat mixture in pot. Add frozen vegetables and tomatoes. Bring to boiling; reduce heat. Simmer, uncovered, 5 minutes or until most of the liquid is evaporated.

3. Meanwhile, unroll pizza dough; cut into 1-inch strips. Arrange strips on top of the meat mixture in pot, trimming to fit. If desired, brush dough with lightly beaten egg.

4. Bake, uncovered, 15 to 20 minutes or until golden.

TO MAKE AHEAD: Prepare as directed through Step 2. Place filling in an airtight container; cool slightly. Cover and refrigerate up to 3 days. To serve, return filling to pot. Cook, covered, over medium heat until heated through, stirring occasionally. Continue as directed in Step 3.

PER SERVING: 511 cal., 15 g fat (5 g sat. fat), 74 mg chol., 1,284 mg sodium, 62 g carb., 6 g fiber, 10 g sugars, 34 g pro.

cheeseburger shepherd's pie

PREP: 30 minutes | **BAKE:** 20 minutes at 350°F | **MAKES:** 6 servings (1 cup each)

Nonstick cooking spray

1½ lb. ground chicken, ground turkey, or ground beef

½ cup chopped red and/or green sweet pepper

⅓ cup chopped onion

2 tsp. minced garlic

1½ cups frozen whole kernel corn

¾ cup water

1 6-oz. can tomato paste with Italian herbs

½ cup coarsely chopped dill pickles or ¼ cup dill pickle relish

¼ cup yellow mustard

1 cup shredded cheddar cheese (4 oz.)

1 24-oz. container refrigerated mashed potatoes

Sliced green onions and/or chopped pickles (optional)

1. Preheat oven to 350°F. Coat an oven-safe 4- to 5-qt. pot with cooking spray. Cook the next four ingredients (through garlic) in the pot over medium-high heat until meat is browned. Drain off any fat.

2. Stir the next five ingredients (through mustard) into meat mixture in pot. Bring to boiling; reduce heat. Simmer, uncovered, 5 minutes to blend flavors. Stir in ½ cup of the cheese. Spoon mashed potatoes in mounds onto meat mixture. Sprinkle with the remaining ½ cup cheese.

3. Bake, uncovered, 20 minutes or until heated through and cheese is melted. If desired, top with green onions and/or pickles.

PER SERVING: 441 cal., 22 g fat (10 g sat. fat), 134 mg chol., 1,042 mg sodium, 33 g carb., 5 g fiber, 8 g sugars, 30 g pro.

MEXICAN SHEPHERD'S PIE: Add ½ cup salsa with the tomato paste. Omit pickles.

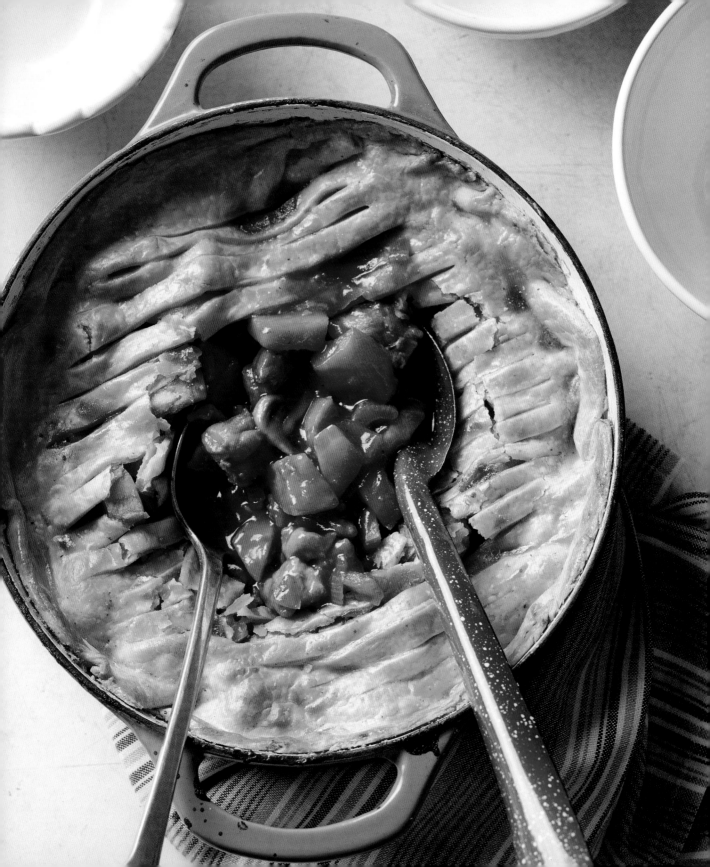

barbecue chicken pot pie

PREP: 45 minutes | **BAKE:** 20 minutes at 450°F | **STAND:** 5 minutes | **MAKES:** 6 servings (1 cup each)

2 Tbsp. olive oil

2 cups chopped, peeled sweet potatoes or Yukon gold potatoes

1 8-oz. pkg. sliced button mushrooms (3 cups)

½ cup chopped onion

½ cup chopped celery

½ cup chopped, peeled carrots or parsnips

1¼ lb. skinless, boneless chicken thighs, cut into ¾-inch pieces

1 cup bottled barbecue sauce

½ of a 14.1-oz. pkg. rolled refrigerated unbaked piecrust (1 crust)

1 egg, lightly beaten (optional)

1. Preheat oven to 450°F. In an oven-safe 3½- or 4-qt. pot heat 1 Tbsp. of the oil over medium-high heat. Add the next five ingredients (through carrots); cook 10 to 12 minutes or until tender, stirring occasionally. Remove vegetables from pot.

2. In the same pot cook and stir chicken in the remaining 1 Tbsp. oil over medium-high heat 5 to 7 minutes or until no longer pink. Return vegetables to pot. Stir in barbecue sauce. Heat until bubbly.

3. Meanwhile, unroll piecrust. Cut slits for steam to escape. Gently place piecrust on chicken mixture in pot, tucking edge into side of pot. If desired, brush crust with lightly beaten egg.

4. Bake, uncovered, 20 minutes or until the filling is bubbly and crust is golden brown. Let stand 5 minutes before serving.

TO MAKE AHEAD: Prepare as directed through Step 2. Place filling in an airtight container; cool slightly. Cover and refrigerate up to 3 days. To serve, return filling to pot. Cook, covered, over medium heat until heated through, stirring occasionally. Continue as directed in Step 3.

PER SERVING: *416 cal., 17 g fat (5 g sat. fat), 92 mg chol., 732 mg sodium, 46 g carb., 3 g fiber, 18 g sugars, 22 g pro.*

easy turkey-pesto pot pie

PREP: 15 minutes | **BAKE:** 20 minutes at 375°F | **MAKES:** 6 servings (1 cup each)

1   18-oz. jar turkey gravy*

¼   cup purchased basil pesto

3   cups cubed cooked turkey
    (about 1 lb.)

1   16-oz. pkg. frozen peas and
    carrots or frozen carrots,
    onions, potatoes, and celery

1   11-oz. pkg. refrigerated
    breadsticks (8 to
    12 breadsticks)

1. Preheat oven to 375°F. In an oven-safe 4-qt. pot combine gravy and pesto; stir in turkey and vegetables. Bring to boiling, stirring frequently. Unroll and separate breadsticks. Arrange breadsticks on top of turkey mixture in pot.

2. Bake, uncovered, about 20 minutes or until breadsticks are golden brown.

*TIP: If you can't find the 18-oz. jar of gravy, use one and a half 12-oz. jars.

PER SERVING: 375 cal., 11 g fat (2 g sat. fat), 76 mg chol., 1,091 mg sodium, 40 g carb., 4 g fiber, 4 g sugars, 30 g pro.

easy pumpkin mac and cheese

PREP: 5 minutes | **COOK:** 20 minutes | **STAND:** 5 minutes | **MAKES:** 6 servings (1⅓ cups each)

- 1 16-oz. pkg. dried rotini or penne pasta
- 1 15- to 16-oz. jar Alfredo pasta sauce
- 1 15-oz. can pumpkin
- ½ cup chopped bottled roasted red sweet peppers
- 4 cups water
- ¼ tsp. salt
- ⅛ tsp. cracked black pepper
- 1½ cups shredded Fontina cheese (6 oz.)

1. In a 5- to 6-qt. nonstick pot combine the first seven ingredients (through black pepper). Stir in ½ cup of the cheese. Bring to boiling over medium-high heat, stirring frequently. Reduce heat to medium. Simmer, covered, 20 minutes or until pasta is tender, stirring frequently. Remove pot from heat. Sprinkle with the remaining 1 cup cheese. Cover; let stand 5 minutes before serving. Serve with additional cracked black pepper.

PER SERVING: 538 cal., 21 g fat (12 g sat. fat), 92 mg chol., 872 mg sodium, 67 g carb., 5 g fiber, 7 g sugars, 20 g pro.

 | FAST PREP

cheesy tuna noodle casserole

PREP: 30 minutes | BAKE: 30 minutes at 375°F | STAND: 5 minutes | MAKES: 6 servings (1⅓ cups each)

3 cups dried wide noodles (6 oz.)

¼ cup butter

1 cup chopped red sweet pepper

1 cup chopped celery

¼ cup chopped onion

¼ cup all-purpose flour

1 to 2 Tbsp. Dijon-style mustard

½ tsp. salt

¼ tsp. black pepper

3 cups milk

1 12-oz. can or two 5-oz. pouches chunk white tuna (water pack), drained

6 oz. cheddar cheese, cut into ¼-inch cubes

½ cup panko bread crumbs

1 Tbsp. butter, melted

1. Preheat oven to 375°F. In an oven-safe 6-qt. pot cook noodles according to package directions; drain in a colander. Set noodles aside. Wipe out pot.

2. In the same pot melt the ¼ cup butter over medium heat. Add sweet pepper, celery, and onion; cook 8 to 10 minutes or until tender, stirring occasionally. Stir in flour, mustard, salt, and black pepper. Gradually stir in milk. Cook and stir until slightly thickened and bubbly. Gently stir in tuna, cheese, and the cooked noodles. In a small bowl stir together panko and the 1 Tbsp. melted butter until evenly coated. Sprinkle over casserole.

3. Bake, uncovered, 30 to 35 minutes or until topping is golden brown. Let stand 5 minutes before serving.

PER SERVING: *473 cal., 24 g fat (14 g sat. fat), 105 mg chol., 766 mg sodium, 37 g carb., 2 g fiber, 9 g sugars, 26 g pro.*

pork cassoulet

PREP: 30 minutes | BAKE: 25 minutes at 350°F | MAKES: 4 to 6 servings (1½ cups each)

1   Tbsp. olive oil

½   cup chopped onion

½   cup chopped carrot

½   cup thinly sliced celery

1   lb. pork tenderloin, trimmed and cut into 1-inch pieces

6   oz. smoked turkey sausage, thinly sliced

2   15.8-oz. cans reduced-sodium Great Northern beans, rinsed and drained

⅔   cup chopped roma tomatoes

½   cup reduced-sodium chicken broth

2   Tbsp. tomato paste

1   Tbsp. white wine vinegar or lemon juice

1   tsp. dried Italian seasoning, crushed

2   Tbsp. snipped fresh Italian parsley

Salt and black pepper

1. Preheat oven to 350°F. In an oven-safe 3- to 4-qt. pot heat oil over medium heat. Add onion, carrot, and celery; cook 5 minutes, stirring occasionally. Add pork and sausage; cook 5 minutes more or until browned.

2. Mash half of the beans. Stir the mashed beans, remaining beans, and the next five ingredients (through Italian seasoning) into meat mixture in pot.

3. Bake, covered, 25 minutes or until pork is tender. Sprinkle with parsley. Season to taste salt and pepper.

PER SERVING: *417 cal., 10 g fat (2 g sat. fat), 96 mg chol., 938 mg sodium, 39 g carb., 10 g fiber, 4 g sugars, 43 g pro.*

WHAT IS CASSOULET?

This low-and-slow-cooked dish hails from France's Languedoc region. Although it varies according to preference and location, it typically includes a mixture of white beans and various meats such as sausage, pork, and/or duck.

WANT TO CUT THE SODIUM? NO PROBLEM. YOU CAN OMIT THE PEPPERONI, CUT DOWN THE CHEESE TO ½ CUP, AND USE NO-SALT-ADDED TOMATO SAUCE.

upside-down pizza casserole

PREP: 20 minutes | **BAKE:** 15 minutes at 400°F | **MAKES:** 5 servings (¾ cup casserole + 2 biscuits each)

1 lb. lean ground beef

1 5-oz. pkg. mini pepperoni slices or chopped pepperoni (optional)

¾ cup chopped green sweet pepper

1 15-oz. can tomato sauce

1 4-oz. can sliced mushrooms, drained

1 2.25-oz. can sliced pitted ripe olives, drained

¼ cup water

1 tsp. Italian seasoning, crushed

1 cup shredded mozzarella cheese (4 oz.)

1 7.5-oz. pkg. refrigerated biscuits (10 biscuits)

1. Preheat oven to 400°F. In an oven-safe 6-qt. pot cook and stir beef, pepperoni (if using), and green pepper over medium-high heat until browned. Drain off fat.

2. Stir in the next five ingredients (through Italian seasoning). Heat through. Sprinkle with ¾ cup of the cheese. Cut each biscuit into four wedges. Arrange the biscuit pieces around the edge of the pot. Sprinkle with the remaining ¼ cup cheese.

3. Bake, uncovered, 15 to 18 minutes or until biscuits are golden.

PER SERVING: *378 cal., 18 g fat (7 g sat. fat), 73 mg chol., 1,156 mg sodium, 27 g carb., 3 g fiber, 7 g sugars, 28 g pro.*

smoked turkey and potato casserole

PREP: 25 minutes | **SLOW COOK:** 8 to 10 hours (low) or 4 to 5 hours (high) + 15 minutes (high)
MAKES: 9 servings (1 cup each)

2 lb. medium round red potatoes, quartered

½ cup sliced celery

½ cup reduced-sodium chicken broth

½ tsp. salt

¼ tsp. black pepper

1 bunch green onions (6), thinly sliced, green and white parts separated

1 smoked turkey drumstick (about 1¾ lb.) (tip, *right*)

¾ cup half-and-half

¼ cup freshly grated Parmesan cheese

2 Tbsp. all-purpose flour

1 Tbsp. dry sherry (optional)

½ cup frozen green peas, thawed

1. In a 5- to 6-qt. slow cooker combine the first five ingredients (through pepper) and the white parts of the green onions. Place turkey drumstick on top of potato mixture in cooker.

2. Cover and cook on low 8 to 10 hours or on high 4 to 5 hours or until potatoes are tender.

3. Remove drumstick from cooker. Let cool slightly. When cool enough to handle, remove meat from bone; discard skin and bone. Coarsely chop turkey and return to cooker.

4. In a medium bowl whisk together half-and-half, cheese, flour, and, if desired, sherry. Stir the half-and-half mixture and the peas into the potato mixture in cooker. If using low, turn cooker to high. Cover and cook 15 minutes more. Top servings with green parts of green onions.

PER SERVING: *111 cal., 4 g fat (2 g sat. fat), 25 mg chol., 356 mg sodium, 10 g carb., 1 g fiber, 1 g sugars, 9 g pro.*

HAM IT UP

If you prefer, you can swap out the smoked turkey leg for a smoked ham hock, which will lend a similar deep, savory flavor.

Creamy Vegetable-Tortellini Soup, *page 147*

soup's
on

When you're craving steamy-hot
soup—but also tight on kitchen time—
these stir-and-go slow cooker soups and
unbelievably quick stove-top simmers
will get dinner on the table fast.

lasagna soup

PREP: 20 minutes | **COOK:** 20 minutes | **MAKES:** 6 servings (1¾ cups each)

6   **to 8 cups reduced-sodium chicken broth**

1   **14.5-oz. can no-salt-added diced tomatoes, undrained**

2   **8-oz. cans no-salt-added tomato sauce**

½   **cup chopped onion**

½   **cup chopped green sweet pepper**

2   **tsp. dried Italian seasoning, crushed**

3   **cloves garlic, minced**

1   **lb. uncooked bulk Italian turkey sausage or ground turkey**

10   **oz. whole wheat or regular lasagna noodles, broken into bite-size pieces**

  Part-skim ricotta cheese (optional)

  Finely shredded Parmesan cheese (optional)

1. In a large pot combine 6 cups broth and the next six ingredients (through garlic). Bring to boiling; reduce heat.

2. Drop spoonfuls of uncooked sausage into the broth mixture until all is added. Add lasagna noodles. Simmer gently, covered, 20 minutes or until noodles are tender, stirring occasionally. If needed, add additional broth to reach desired consistency. If desired, top servings with ricotta and Parmesan cheese.

PER SERVING: *342 cal., 8 g fat (2 g sat. fat), 42 mg chol., 1,075 mg sodium, 47 g carb., 8 g fiber, 9 g sugars, 23 g pro.*

FAST PREP

mushroom and beef ravioli soup

START TO FINISH: 20 minutes | **MAKES:** 4 servings (1½ cups each)

- 1 Tbsp. olive oil
- 1 small onion, halved and thinly sliced
- 2 cups sliced cremini mushrooms (6 oz.)
- 2 miniature red sweet peppers, stemmed and sliced (about ½ cup)
- 1 32-oz. box mushroom or beef broth
- 1 20-oz. pkg. frozen beef ravioli
- Fresh thyme leaves
- Black pepper

1. In a 4-qt. pot heat olive oil over medium-high heat. Add onion slices, mushrooms, and sweet peppers; cook and stir 4 minutes or until tender. Stir in broth; bring to boiling. Stir in ravioli; return to boiling. Reduce heat. Cook, uncovered, 5 to 8 minutes or until pasta is tender, stirring occasionally. Sprinkle with thyme and black pepper before serving.

PER SERVING: 357 cal., 12 g fat (4 g sat. fat), 64 mg chol., 645 mg sodium, 45 g carb., 3 g fiber, 5 g sugars, 16 g pro.

creamy vegetable-tortellini soup *pictured on page 142*

PREP: 15 minutes | **COOK:** 7 minutes | **MAKES:** 6 servings (1¼ cups each)

- 2 14.5-oz. cans reduced-sodium chicken or vegetable broth
- 1 15-oz. jar Alfredo pasta sauce
- 1 9-oz. pkg. refrigerated cheese-filled tortellini
- 1¼ cups chopped yellow summer squash
- ½ cup halved cherry tomatoes
- ⅓ cup purchased basil pesto

1. In a 4-qt. pot combine first five ingredients (through tomatoes). Bring to boiling; reduce heat. Simmer 7 to 9 minutes or just until squash and tortellini are tender, stirring occasionally. Before serving, stir in pesto.

PER SERVING: *329 cal., 20 g fat (8 g sat. fat), 80 mg chol., 1,115 mg sodium, 27 g carb., 2 g fiber, 5 g sugars, 12 g pro.*

turkey noodle soup

PREP: 15 minutes | **COOK:** 35 minutes | **MAKES:** 6 to 8 servings (2 cups each)

- 2   32-oz. boxes chicken broth
- 1   14.5-oz. can fire-roasted diced tomatoes, undrained
- 1   cup frozen sweet or roasted corn kernels
- 1   cup frozen sweet peas
- 1   cup sliced carrots
- ½   cup sliced celery
- ½   cup thin onion wedges
- 1   tsp. dried thyme, crushed
- 2   cups dried egg noodles
- 2   cups chopped cooked turkey

1. In a 4- to 6-qt. pot combine first eight ingredients (through thyme). Bring to boiling; reduce heat. Simmer, covered, about 30 minutes or until vegetables are tender. Add noodles and turkey. Return to boiling. Cook 5 to 7 minutes or until noodles are tender, stirring occasionally.

PER SERVING: *244 cal., 4 g fat (1 g sat. fat), 80 mg chol., 643 mg sodium, 27 g carb., 4 g fiber, 7 g sugars, 26 g pro.*

hearty italian zoup

PREP: 20 minutes | **COOK:** 15 minutes | **MAKES:** 6 servings (1½ cups each)

1   medium zucchini

1   Tbsp. olive oil

3   links uncooked Italian turkey sausage (about 12 oz.), casings removed

½   cup chopped onion

½   cup coarsely shredded carrot

2   cloves garlic, minced

2   14.5-oz. cans reduced-sodium chicken broth

1   14.5-oz. can petite diced tomatoes, undrained

1   15-oz. can cannellini beans (white kidney beans), rinsed and drained

4   cups torn escarole or fresh baby spinach

1   Tbsp. snipped fresh marjoram or oregano

Salt and black pepper

1   Tbsp. red wine vinegar (optional)

Finely shredded Asiago cheese

1. For zucchini noodles, trim stem and blossom ends from zucchini. Use a spiralizer to cut zucchini into spaghetti-size noodles.* If desired, cut into shorter lengths.

2. In a 6-qt. pot heat oil over medium heat. Add sausage, onion, carrot, and garlic. Cook and stir 5 to 8 minutes or until sausage is browned and vegetables are tender. Add broth and tomatoes. Bring to boiling. Add zucchini noodles, beans, escarole, and marjoram. Return to boiling; reduce heat. Simmer, uncovered, 4 minutes or just until zucchini noodles are tender and escarole is wilted. If desired, stir in vinegar. Season to taste with salt and pepper. Top servings with Asiago cheese.

*TIP: If you don't have a spiralizer, cut zucchini into 2-inch-long matchstick pieces and continue as directed.

PER SERVING: 227 cal., 10 g fat (3 g sat. fat), 41 mg chol., 1,255 mg sodium, 18 g carb., 6 g fiber, 4 g sugars, 17 g pro.

pork and wild rice soup

PREP: 15 minutes | **COOK:** 10 minutes | **MAKES:** 6 servings (1⅓ cups each)

1 32-oz. box reduced-sodium chicken broth

2 8.8-oz. pouches cooked long grain and wild rice

1 15-oz. pkg. refrigerated cooked pork roast au jus, broken into chunks

½ oz. dried porcini or oyster mushrooms, broken and rinsed (tip, *right*)

1 Tbsp. snipped fresh sage or 1 tsp. dried sage, crushed

1. In a 4-qt. pot combine all of the ingredients. Bring just to boiling; reduce heat. Simmer, covered, 10 minutes, stirring occasionally.

2. If desired, top servings with additional fresh sage.

PER SERVING: 219 cal., 5 g fat (2 g sat. fat), 38 mg chol., 1,065 mg sodium, 24 g carb., 1 g fiber, 1 g sugars, 18 g pro.

ABOUT DRIED MUSHROOMS

Dried mushrooms pack a lot of flavor into a small package, lending a deep, earthy taste to soups and sauces. Look for them near dried vegetables or spices in larger grocery stores or at specialty food stores and Italian markets. Be sure to rinse dried mushrooms thoroughly before adding them to the soup—they often contain grit or dirt that wasn't washed off before drying.

lentil-chard soup

PREP: 15 minutes | **COOK:** 15 minutes | **MAKES:** 6 servings (1⅔ cups each)

4 cups coarsely chopped Swiss chard

1 32-oz. box reduced-sodium chicken broth

1 14-oz. pkg. frozen mirepoix (carrots, celery, and onion) or one 16-oz. pkg. frozen stew vegetables

1 9-oz. pkg. refrigerated steamed lentils

1¾ cups water

1½ cups diced cooked ham

1 tsp. dried Italian seasoning, crushed

Baguette garlic toasts* (optional)

Finely shredded Parmesan cheese (optional)

1. In a 4-qt. pot combine first seven ingredients (through Italian seasoning). Bring to boiling; reduce heat. Simmer 15 minutes or until vegetables are tender, stirring occasionally.

2. If desired, serve with baguette garlic toasts and Parmesan cheese.

PER SERVING: 155 cal., 3 g fat (1 g sat. fat), 20 mg chol., 950 mg sodium, 19 g carb., 5 g fiber, 4 g sugars, 13 g pro.

*TIP: For garlic toasts, toast slices of baguette-style French bread in a 375°F oven until golden. While warm, rub with a halved garlic clove.

| FAST PREP

fennel and bean ham-bone soup

PREP: 30 minutes | SOAK: 1 hour | COOK: 1 hour | MAKES: 8 servings (1 cup each)

1 lb. dried Great Northern beans

2 Tbsp. butter

1 1- to 1½-lb. meaty ham bone or 1 to 1½ lb. meaty smoked pork hocks

½ tsp. salt

½ tsp. black pepper

2 medium fennel bulbs, trimmed, cored, and cut into thin wedges (tip, *right*)

2 cups fresh green beans, trimmed and halved crosswise, or frozen cut green beans

2 cups thinly sliced carrots

2 Tbsp. snipped fresh oregano and/or thyme

2 Tbsp. balsamic vinegar

1. Rinse dried beans; drain. In a 5-qt. pot combine beans and 8 cups water. Bring to boiling; reduce heat. Simmer, uncovered, 2 minutes. Remove from heat. Cover and let stand 1 hour. (Or place beans in water in the pot. Let soak in a cool place overnight.) Drain and rinse beans; set beans aside.

2. In the same pot melt butter over medium heat. Add ham bone and brown on all sides. Stir in Great Northern beans, salt, pepper, and 8 cups fresh water. Bring to boiling; reduce heat. Simmer, covered, 1 to 1½ hours or until beans are tender, adding fennel, green beans, and carrots for the last 30 minutes of cooking.

3. Remove ham bone. When cool enough to handle, cut meat off bone. Coarsely chop meat. Add meat and oregano to soup in pot. Remove from heat. Stir in vinegar just before serving.

PER SERVING: *264 cal., 6 g fat (3 g sat. fat), 20 mg chol., 269 mg sodium, 39 g carb., 11 g fiber, 4 g sugars, 16 g pro.*

ALL ABOUT FENNEL

Fennel has a light but distinct licoricelike flavor that mellows and sweetens when cooked. When buying fennel, look for firm, plump bulbs with fresh greenery that has no signs of browning or wilting. To prepare fennel, trim it about 1 inch above the bulb, then cut it lengthwise into quarters. Cut away the core from each piece and then slice into wedges. Save some of the bright green fronds for garnish.

creamy corn soup with crispy bacon

PREP: 25 minutes | **COOK:** 45 minutes | **COOL:** 10 minutes | **MAKES:** 4 servings (1¼ cups each)

- 2 Tbsp. unsalted butter
- 1 cup chopped onion
- ½ tsp. salt
- 4 cups frozen whole kernel corn
- ½ cup thinly sliced carrot
- ½ cup thinly sliced celery
- 2 cloves garlic, minced
- 2 cups reduced-sodium chicken broth
- 2 cups milk
- 2 sprigs fresh thyme or ½ tsp. dried thyme, crushed
- 2 bay leaves
- 2 slices bacon, crisp-cooked and crumbled

  Cracked black pepper

1. In a 4-qt. pot melt butter over medium heat. Add onion and salt; cook and stir 5 minutes or until onion is tender.

2. Add corn, carrot, celery, and garlic; cook about 10 minutes or until vegetables are soft, stirring frequently. If desired, set aside about ½ cup of the cooked vegetables to use as a garnish.

3. Add broth, milk, thyme, and bay leaves to vegetable mixture in pot. Bring to boiling; reduce heat. Simmer, covered, 30 minutes, stirring occasionally.

4. Remove soup from heat; cool 10 minutes. Remove and discard thyme sprigs (if present) and bay leaves. Using an immersion blender, blend soup until smooth. (Or transfer part of the soup to a blender; cover and blend until smooth. Repeat with the remaining soup, blending in batches. Return all of the soup to the pot.) Heat through. Top servings with reserved vegetables (if using) and crumbled bacon; sprinkle with cracked pepper.

PER SERVING: 233 cal., 10 g fat (6 g sat. fat), 28 mg chol., 781 mg sodium, 29 g carb., 3 g fiber, 15 g sugars, 11 g pro.

cajun sausage-potato soup

PREP: 20 minutes | **COOK:** 10 minutes | **MAKES:** 6 servings (1⅓ cups each)

4 cups frozen diced hash brown potatoes with onions and peppers

1 14.5-oz. can reduced-sodium chicken broth

1 13.5- to 14-oz. pkg. cooked andouille or other smoked sausage, chopped

1 10.75-oz. can condensed cream of celery soup

1 cup water

2 tsp. Cajun seasoning

½ cup heavy cream

Sliced green onions (optional)

1. In a 4-qt. pot combine the first six ingredients (through Cajun seasoning). Bring to boiling; reduce heat. Simmer 10 minutes or until potatoes are tender, stirring occasionally.

2. Before serving, stir in cream. If desired, top servings with green onions.

PER SERVING: *363 cal., 26 g fat (11 g sat. fat), 67 mg chol., 1,113 mg sodium, 20 g carb., 2 g fiber, 1 g sugars, 12 g pro.*

chicken taco tortilla soup

PREP: 15 minutes | **COOK:** 5 minutes | **MAKES:** 6 servings (1⅓ cups each)

2 cups shredded rotisserie chicken

2 cups water

1 15.5- to 16-oz. jar black bean and corn salsa

1 14.5-oz. can reduced-sodium chicken broth

1 12-oz. pkg. frozen fire-roasted tricolor peppers, such as Green Giant*

2 tsp. dried oregano, crushed

Coarsely crushed tortilla chips (optional)

Sour cream (optional)

1. In a 4-qt. pot combine first six ingredients (through oregano). Bring to boiling; reduce heat. Simmer 5 minutes or until heated through, stirring occasionally.

2. If desired, top servings with tortilla chips and sour cream.

*TIP: If you can't find frozen fire-roasted peppers, substitute one 14.4-oz. pkg. frozen pepper stir-fry vegetables (green, red, and yellow sweet peppers and onions).

PER SERVING: 217 cal., 7 g fat (1 g sat. fat), 53 mg chol., 737 mg sodium, 25 g carb., 6 g fiber, 4 g sugars, 17 g pro.

chicken lentil-farro bowl

PREP: 25 minutes | **COOK:** 30 minutes | **MAKES:** 6 servings (1⅓ cups each)

7	to 8 cups chicken broth
⅔	cup pearled farro
½	cup dried French lentils
1	Tbsp. olive oil
1½	cups coarsely chopped fennel bulb (1 medium)
3	carrots, halved lengthwise and cut up
2	small leeks, trimmed and sliced
3	Tbsp. snipped fresh parsley
3	Tbsp. snipped fresh fennel fronds (optional)
2	cloves garlic, minced
2	cups shredded cooked chicken
½	tsp. salt
½	tsp. black pepper
	Lemon slices (optional)

1. In a 4-qt. pot bring broth to boiling. Add farro and lentils. Return to boiling; reduce heat. Simmer 25 to 30 minutes or until tender.

2. Meanwhile, in a large skillet heat oil over medium heat. Add chopped fennel, carrots, and leeks; cook about 5 minutes or until tender. In a small bowl stir together parsley, fennel fronds (if using), and garlic.

3. Stir sautéed vegetables, chicken, salt, and pepper into broth mixture. Cook and stir until heated through. If desired, float a lemon slice on each serving; top with parsley mixture.

PER SERVING: *312 cal., 7 g fat (2 g sat. fat), 61 mg chol., 613 mg sodium, 35 g carb., 6 g fiber, 4 g sugars, 28 g pro.*

THE EASIEST WAY TO GRATE FRESH GINGER? FREEZE IT FIRST! WHEN FROZEN, THE FIBERS WON'T GET STUCK IN YOUR GRATER.

jamaican pepper pot

PREP: 30 minutes | **COOK:** 15 minutes | **MAKES:** 6 servings (1½ cups each)

1   Tbsp. vegetable oil

½   cup chopped onion

1   Tbsp. grated fresh ginger

1   fresh habanero or serrano chile pepper, seeded and minced (tip, *page 14*)

2   cloves garlic, minced

2   14.5-oz. cans reduced-sodium chicken broth

1   lb. sweet potatoes, peeled and cut into ½-inch chunks

1   14- to 16-oz. pkg. frozen meatballs

1   tsp. snipped fresh thyme

5   cups baby spinach

1   13.5-oz. can unsweetened coconut milk

1   cup frozen sliced okra*

¼   tsp. salt

     Toasted unsweetened flaked coconut

     Lime wedges

1. In a 4-qt. pot heat oil over medium heat. Add the next four ingredients (through garlic); cook and stir until tender.

2. Add next four ingredients (through thyme) and bring to boiling; reduce heat. Simmer, uncovered, 15 minutes or until sweet potatoes are tender. Add spinach, coconut milk, okra, and salt. Cook 2 to 3 minutes more or until heated through and spinach is just wilted. Top servings with coconut. Serve with lime wedges.

*TIP: If using fresh okra, remove and discard the stems; slice the okra. Add to pot with the sweet potatoes.

PER SERVING: *444 cal., 32 g fat (18 g sat. fat), 23 mg chol., 1,033 mg sodium, 27 g carb., 6 g fiber, 6 g sugars, 13 g pro.*

spring lamb and fava bean soup

PREP: 20 minutes | **SLOW COOK:** 8¼ to 10¼ hours (low) or 4¼ to 5¼ hours (high)
MAKES: 8 servings (1¼ cups each)

1 Tbsp. olive oil

1 lb. boneless lamb shoulder or beef chuck, trimmed of fat and cut into 1-inch pieces

1 32-oz. box beef broth

1½ cups water

8 oz. morel, oyster, or cremini mushrooms, sliced

1 8.8-oz. pkg. peeled and steamed fava beans, rinsed and drained, or 1½ cups frozen fava beans, thawed (tip, *right*)

1 cup sliced carrots

2 medium leeks, sliced

⅓ cup regular pearled barley

1 tsp. snipped fresh thyme

1 tsp. snipped fresh rosemary

1 cup shelled fresh English peas or frozen peas, thawed

Salt and black pepper

1 recipe Lemon Gremolata (optional)

1. In a large skillet heat oil over medium heat. Add lamb; cook until browned. Drain off fat.

2. In a 4- to 5-qt. slow cooker combine lamb and the next nine ingredients (through rosemary).

3. Cover and cook on low 8 to 10 hours or on high 4 to 5 hours. Stir in peas. Cook 15 minutes more. Season to taste with salt and pepper. If desired, top servings with Lemon Gremolata.

PER SERVING: *206 cal., 6 g fat (2 g sat. fat), 42 mg chol., 314 mg sodium, 20 g carb., 5 g fiber, 4 g sugars, 19 g pro.*

LEMON GREMOLATA: In a small bowl combine ¼ cup snipped fresh Italian parsley, 1 Tbsp. lemon zest, and 2 cloves garlic, minced.

FABULOUS FAVAS

Prized in Mediterranean and Middle Eastern cooking, these giant green, limalike beans have a bright, fresh, grassy flavor. Each bean has a very tough skin that needs to be removed before cooking, which can make them labor-intensive to prepare. This recipe calls for packaged favas, which are peeled and ready to use.

curried vegetable soup with quinoa and tempeh

START TO FINISH: 40 minutes | **MAKES:** 6 servings (1⅓ cups each)

1 Tbsp. olive oil

1 8-oz. pkg. tempeh (fermented soybean cake), cut into ½-inch cubes (tip, *right*)

1 medium leek (white part only), halved lengthwise and thinly sliced (about ⅓ cup)

1 Tbsp. curry powder

1 32-oz. box vegetable broth

1 14.5-oz. can diced fire-roasted tomatoes, undrained

1 cup water

1½ cups kale or Swiss chard, stems removed and leaves coarsely chopped

½ cup quinoa, rinsed and drained

½ cup sliced carrot

½ cup frozen whole kernel corn

⅓ cup snipped fresh basil

Salt

1. In a 3-qt. pot heat 1½ tsp. of the oil over medium-high heat. Add tempeh; cook about 7 minutes or until golden, stirring occasionally. Remove tempeh from pot.

2. In the same pot heat the remaining 1½ tsp. oil over medium heat. Add leek; cook 2 to 4 minutes or until tender, stirring occasionally. Stir in curry powder. Add broth, tomatoes, and the water. Bring to boiling. Stir in kale, quinoa, and carrot. Return to boiling; reduce heat. Simmer, covered, 15 minutes. Stir in tempeh and corn. Simmer, covered, until quinoa is tender and tempeh is heated through.

3. Remove pot from heat. Stir in basil. Season to taste with salt.

PER SERVING: *200 cal., 8 g fat (1 g sat. fat), 0 mg chol., 784 mg sodium, 24 g carb., 3 g fiber, 5 g sugars, 11 g pro.*

WHAT IS TEMPEH?

This vegetarian meat alternative is fermented soybean cake that is high in protein and low in fat and cholesterol. Its yeasty, nutty flavor plus its dense, firm, and pleasantly chewy texture make it a great stand-in for meat in soups, casseroles, and more. Look for it in the health food section of your grocery store or at natural food stores.

pumpkin, barley, and andouille soup

START TO FINISH: 35 minutes | **MAKES:** 4 servings (1½ cups each)

1 Tbsp. vegetable oil

8 oz. cooked andouille or smoked sausage links, halved lengthwise and sliced

⅓ cup chopped onion

1 32-oz. box reduced-sodium chicken broth

1 cup quick-cooking barley

1 Tbsp. snipped fresh sage or 1 tsp. dried sage, crushed

1 15-oz. can pumpkin

2 Tbsp. maple syrup

1 Tbsp. cider vinegar

Salt and black pepper

1. In a 4-qt. pot heat oil over medium heat. Add sausage and onion; cook 3 minutes, stirring frequently. Add broth, barley, and, if using, dried sage.

2. Bring to boiling; reduce heat. Simmer, covered, 12 minutes, stirring occasionally. Stir in pumpkin, maple syrup, and vinegar. Cook until heated through, stirring occasionally.

3. Stir in fresh sage (if using). Season to taste with salt and pepper. If desired, top servings with additional fresh sage.

PER SERVING: *398 cal., 19 g fat (6 g sat. fat), 35 mg chol., 749 mg sodium, 46 g carb., 7 g fiber, 10 g sugars, 14 g pro.*

Pacific Salmon Chowder, *page 189*

stew
about it

Grab your biggest spoon and rediscover your love for stews
and chowders with these extraordinary—and totally doable—
pots of slow-simmered goodness.

autumn beef stew

PREP: 45 minutes | **COOK:** 2 hours | **MAKES:** 8 servings (1¾ cups each)

¼ cup all-purpose flour

1½ tsp. kosher salt

1 tsp. cracked black pepper

2 lb. boneless beef chuck, trimmed of fat and cut into 1½-inch chunks

2 slices bacon, cut crosswise into ¼-inch strips

Canola oil

2 medium onions, cut into ½-inch wedges

4 cloves garlic, minced

2 Tbsp. tomato paste

5 cups reduced-sodium chicken broth

2 cups reduced-sodium beef broth

1½ cups dry red wine

1 Tbsp. snipped fresh thyme

1 tsp. smoked paprika

1 lb. potatoes, cut into 2-inch chunks

1 lb. butternut squash, peeled, seeded, and cut into 1½-inch chunks

4 carrots, cut into 1-inch pieces

2 stalks celery, sliced ½ inch thick

¼ cup chopped fresh Italian parsley

1. In a large plastic bag combine flour, salt, and pepper. Add beef; shake to coat evenly. In a 5- to 6-qt. pot cook and stir bacon over medium-high heat until crisp. Drain bacon on paper towels, reserving drippings in pot. Add enough oil to bacon drippings to equal 2 Tbsp. Add half the beef to drippings in pot, shaking off any excess flour. Cook until browned, stirring occasionally. Remove beef with a slotted spoon. Repeat with remaining beef.

2. If necessary, add 1 Tbsp. oil to pot. Add onions; cook and stir about 4 minutes or until starting to brown. Stir in garlic; cook 1 minute. Stir in tomato paste. Return beef, bacon, and any remaining flour to pot. Stir to combine. Add the next five ingredients (through paprika). Bring to boiling; reduce heat. Simmer, covered, about 1½ hours or until meat is tender, stirring occasionally.

3. Add the next four ingredients (through celery). Return to boiling; reduce heat. Simmer, covered, 15 minutes. Remove lid; simmer, uncovered, about 15 minutes more or until vegetables are tender and liquid is desired consistency. Discard bay leaves. Stir in parsley.

PER SERVING: 334 cal., 7 g fat (2 g sat. fat), 76 mg chol., 844 mg sodium, 27 g carb., 4 g fiber, 5 g sugars, 31 g pro.

spicy ancho beef stew

PREP: 25 minutes | **BAKE:** 4 hours at 300°F | **MAKES:** 8 servings (1½ cups each)

1½ lb. beef stew meat

1 tsp. salt

8 oz. uncooked chorizo sausage or other sausage, casings removed

½ cup chopped onion

4 cloves garlic, minced

½ cup all-purpose flour

2 tsp. ground ancho chile pepper

2 tsp. Mexican-style chili powder or chili powder

1 12-oz. bottle dark Mexican beer, such as Negra Modelo

1 14.5-oz. can diced tomatoes, undrained

2 lb. Yukon gold potatoes, cut into ½-inch pieces

2 large carrots, peeled and cut into ½-inch pieces

Sliced green onions (optional)

1. Preheat oven to 300°F. Season stew meat with salt. In an oven-safe 5- to 6-qt. pot cook sausage over medium-high heat until browned. Transfer to a bowl with a slotted spoon. Add beef in batches to pot and sear until deep brown all over, about 5 minutes per side. Transfer beef to bowl with sausage.

2. Add onion to pot; cook 4 minutes or until lightly browned. Add garlic and cook 1 minute. Stir in flour, ground ancho chile pepper, and chili powder; cook 1 minute. Add beer and tomatoes. Bring to boiling; reduce heat. Simmer, uncovered, 1 minute. Return sausage and beef to pot, pushing beef into the liquid. Stir in potatoes, carrots, and just enough water to cover the vegetables (about 2 cups). Return to boiling. Cover and bake about 4 hours or until vegetables and meat are fork-tender. Spoon off excess fat before serving. If desired, top servings with sliced green onions.

PER SERVING: 391 cal., 15 g fat (6 g sat. fat), 79 mg chol., 894 mg sodium, 32 g carb., 5 g fiber, 4 g sugars, 29 g pro.

sunday dinner stew

START TO FINISH: 25 minutes | **MAKES:** 4 to 6 servings (1¾ cups each)

- 1 lb. tiny red new potatoes, halved or quartered, or 1 lb. sweet potatoes, peeled and cut up (tip, *right*)
- 3 large carrots, halved lengthwise and cut up
- 1 15-oz. pkg. refrigerated cooked beef tips with gravy
- 2 cups water
- 1 bunch green onions, chopped (½ cup)
- 1 cup chopped fresh kale
- Salt and black pepper
- Snipped fresh thyme (optional)

1. In a 4-qt. pot combine first six ingredients (through kale). Bring to boiling over medium-high heat; reduce heat. Simmer, covered, 20 minutes or until vegetables are tender. Season to taste with salt and pepper. If desired, top servings with fresh thyme.

PER SERVING: 260 cal., 8 g fat (3 g sat. fat), 46 mg chol., 604 mg sodium, 30 g carb., 5 g fiber, 7 g sugars, 19 g pro.

GET SWEET

Give this stew a vitamin A boost by using peeled and coarsely chopped sweet potatoes in place of some or all of the red new potatoes.

chipotle chicken and corn stew

PREP: 25 minutes | **COOK:** 35 minutes | **MAKES:** 6 servings (1⅓ cups each)

4 tsp. canola oil

1 lb. skinless, boneless chicken breast halves, cut into bite-size pieces

2 cups frozen whole kernel corn

½ of a 14.4-oz. pkg. frozen pepper and onion stir-fry vegetables

2 14.5-oz. cans reduced-sodium chicken broth

1 14.5-oz. can no-salt-added fire-roasted diced tomatoes, undrained

4 6-inch corn tortillas, torn into small pieces

2 tsp. salt-free Southwestern chipotle seasoning, such as Mrs. Dash

¼ tsp. salt

¾ cup shredded reduced-fat mild cheddar cheese (3 oz.)

¼ cup thinly sliced green onions

1. In a 5- to 6-qt. pot heat 2 tsp. of the oil over medium heat. Add chicken; cook and stir until no longer pink. Remove from pot. Cover and chill until needed.

2. In the same pot heat the remaining 2 tsp. oil over medium-high heat. Add corn and stir-fry vegetables; cook and stir 3 minutes. Stir in the next five ingredients (through salt). Bring to boiling; reduce heat. Simmer, covered, 30 minutes or until tortillas break down and broth is slightly thick. Stir in chicken. Simmer, uncovered, 5 minutes more. Sprinkle servings with cheese and green onions.

PER SERVING: *279 cal., 9 g fat (3 g sat. fat), 65 mg chol., 577 mg sodium, 25 g carb., 3 g fiber, 5 g sugars, 26 g pro.*

USING BONE-IN CHICKEN PIECES BOOSTS THE RICHNESS OF THE BROTH AND HELPS THE MEAT STAY MOIST AND FLAVORFUL.

african chicken peanut stew

PREP: 30 minutes | **COOK:** 50 minutes | **MAKES:** 6 to 8 servings (1¾ cups each)

  6 green onions
  1 Tbsp. coconut oil or canola
     oil
  1 medium green sweet pepper,
     cut into 1-inch pieces
  1 Tbsp. finely chopped fresh
     ginger
  1 tsp. ground coriander
  ½ tsp. ground cumin
  ½ tsp. crushed red pepper
  4 cloves garlic, minced
  8 medium bone-in chicken
     thighs, skinned (tip, *opposite*)
  3 14.5-oz. cans reduced-
     sodium chicken broth
 12 oz. sweet potatoes, peeled
     and cut into 1-inch chunks
  1 cup coarsely chopped,
     peeled eggplant
  ½ cup creamy peanut butter
  ½ of a 6-oz. can tomato paste
     (⅓ cup)
  1 15-oz. can crushed tomatoes
  ⅓ cup chopped fresh Italian
     parsley
  ½ cup chopped lightly salted
     peanuts

1. Trim ends from green onions; cut off green tops. Cut tops into 2-inch lengths; set aside for serving. Cut white bottoms into 1-inch lengths.

2. In a 6- to 8-qt. pot heat oil over medium heat. Add white parts of green onions and the sweet pepper; cook 5 minutes, stirring occasionally. Add the next five ingredients (through garlic). Cook and stir 30 seconds. Add chicken and broth. Bring to boiling; reduce heat. Simmer, covered, 35 minutes or until chicken is no longer pink (180°F). Transfer chicken to a cutting board. Set aside until cool enough to handle.

3. Add sweet potatoes and eggplant to the pot. Bring to boiling; reduce heat. Simmer, covered, 10 to 15 minutes or until potatoes are tender. Meanwhile, ladle about ½ cup of the hot broth into a medium bowl. Whisk in peanut butter until smooth. Whisk in tomato paste.

4. Remove chicken meat from the bones and coarsely shred the chicken using two forks. Add shredded chicken, peanut butter mixture, and tomatoes to the pot. Cook, covered, over medium-low heat 5 minutes, stirring occasionally. Stir in parsley. Top servings with reserved green onion tops and peanuts.

PER SERVING: 477 cal., 24 g fat (6 g sat. fat), 122 mg chol., 967 mg sodium, 30 g carb., 7 g fiber, 11 g sugars, 39 g pro.

brazilian black bean stew

PREP: 30 minutes | **STAND:** 1 hour | **SLOW COOK:** 8 to 10 hours (low) or 4 to 5 hours (high)
MAKES: 8 servings (1 cup each)

12 oz. dried black beans

2 large smoked ham hocks

4 cups reduced-sodium chicken broth

1½ cups chopped onions

3 fresh jalapeño chile peppers, seeded and minced (tip, *page 14*)

4 cloves garlic, minced

½ cup dry sherry

2 oranges

¼ cup snipped fresh cilantro

Hot cooked rice (optional)

1. Rinse beans. In a large pot combine beans and 8 cups water. Bring to boiling; reduce heat. Simmer, uncovered, 10 minutes. Remove from heat. Cover and let stand 1 hour. (Or place beans in 8 cups water in pot. Cover and let soak in a cool place overnight.) Drain and rinse beans. Place beans in a 4-qt. slow cooker.

2. Add the next six ingredients (through sherry) to slow cooker. Remove 1 Tbsp. zest and squeeze ½ cup juice from the oranges. Add zest and juice to bean mixture in cooker.

3. Cover and cook on low 8 to 10 hours or on high 4 to 5 hours. Transfer ham hocks to a cutting board. When cool enough to handle, use two forks to pull ham away from bones into shreds. Discard bones; return shredded ham to slow cooker. Stir in cilantro. If desired, serve stew over hot cooked rice.

PER SERVING: *253 cal., 5 g fat (2 g sat. fat), 19 mg chol., 333 mg sodium, 34 g carb., 7 g fiber, 5 g sugars, 16 g pro.*

spicy moroccan vegetable stew

PREP: 25 minutes | **COOK:** 45 minutes | **MAKES:** 7 servings (1 cup each)

1 Tbsp. olive oil

1 small bulb fennel, cored and chopped (reserve fronds)

1 cup sliced carrots

¾ cup chopped onion

2 cloves garlic, minced

1½ tsp. grated fresh ginger

½ tsp. salt

½ tsp. ground turmeric

¼ tsp. ground cinnamon

4 cups reduced-sodium vegetable or chicken broth

¾ cup dried lentils

½ cup apple cider or apple juice

1 15-oz. can fire-roasted diced tomatoes, undrained

1 15-oz. can garbanzo beans (chickpeas), rinsed and drained

1. In a 5- to 6-qt. pot heat oil over medium-high heat. Add fennel and carrots; cook and stir 5 minutes. Add onion and garlic; cook and stir 10 to 12 minutes or until vegetables are tender. Add ginger, salt, turmeric, and cinnamon. Cook and stir 1 minute more.

2. Add broth, lentils, and apple cider to vegetable mixture in pot. Bring to boiling; reduce heat. Simmer, covered, 15 minutes. Add tomatoes; simmer 5 to 10 minutes more or until lentils are tender. Add garbanzo beans; heat through. Top servings with fennel fronds.

PER SERVING: 186 cal., 3 g fat (0 g sat. fat), 0 mg chol., 474 mg sodium, 32 g carb., 9 g fiber, 7 g sugars, 9 g pro.

pumpkin-kale calico bean stew

PREP: 15 minutes | **COOK:** 20 minutes | **MAKES:** 8 servings (1⅓ cups each)

- 4 cups vegetable broth
- 1 15-oz. can Great Northern beans, rinsed and drained
- 1 15-oz. can pinto beans, rinsed and drained
- 1 15-oz. can black beans, rinsed and drained
- 1 15-oz. can pumpkin
- 1 14.5-oz. can Italian-style stewed tomatoes, undrained and cut up
- 4 cups coarsely chopped fresh kale (3 oz.)
- 1 cup chopped onion
- 1 cup frozen shelled edamame
- 1 tsp. ground cumin
- 1 tsp. dried oregano, crushed
- 1 tsp. chili powder
- ½ tsp. salt (tip, *right*)
- ½ to 1 cup water
- 1 Tbsp. bottled Louisiana hot sauce (optional)

1. In a 5- to 6-qt. pot combine the first 13 ingredients (through salt). Add the water until stew reaches desired consistency. Bring to boiling over medium-high heat; reduce heat. Simmer, covered, 20 minutes. If desired, serve with hot sauce.

PER SERVING: 199 cal., 2 g fat (0 g sat. fat), 0 mg chol., 1,211 mg sodium, 36 g carb., 12 g fiber, 7 g sugars, 12 g pro.

CUT THE SALT

To reduce the sodium in this soup, omit the ½ teaspoon salt and opt for reduced-sodium chicken broth instead of vegetable broth.

louisiana bayou chowder

PREP: 20 minutes | **COOK:** 30 minutes | **MAKES:** 6 to 8 servings (1⅓ cups each)

1 lb. fresh or frozen peeled, deveined medium shrimp

⅓ cup all-purpose flour

⅓ cup vegetable oil

1 cup chopped onion

½ cup chopped celery

½ cup chopped green sweet pepper

½ cup chopped red sweet pepper

2 cloves garlic, minced

3 cups reduced-sodium chicken broth

2 cups sliced fresh okra or one 10-oz. pkg. frozen sliced okra

¼ tsp. black pepper

⅛ tsp. cayenne pepper

12 oz. cooked andouille sausage or smoked sausage, sliced

1 cup cooked rice

¼ cup chopped green onions

¼ cup heavy cream

1. Thaw shrimp, if frozen. Rinse shrimp; pat dry with paper towels.

2. For roux, in a heavy 4-qt. pot stir together flour and oil until smooth. Cook and stir constantly over medium-high heat about 5 minutes or until the roux is dark reddish brown.

3. Stir the next five ingredients (through garlic) into roux. Cook about 5 minutes or until vegetables are tender, stirring frequently. Add broth, okra, black pepper, and cayenne pepper. Bring to boiling; reduce heat. Simmer, covered, 15 minutes, stirring occasionally.

4. Stir in sausage; heat through. Add shrimp and the remaining ingredients; cook 2 to 4 minutes or until shrimp are opaque, stirring frequently.

PER SERVING: *488 cal., 33 g fat (11 g sat. fat), 164 mg chol., 957 mg sodium, 22 g carb., 3 g fiber, 5 g sugars, 26 g pro.*

manhattan clam chowder

PREP: 15 minutes | **COOK:** 30 minutes | **MAKES:** 4 to 6 servings (1¾ cups each)

1 pint shucked clams or two 6.5-oz. cans minced clams, undrained

4 slices bacon, chopped

1 cup chopped onion

1 cup chopped celery

½ cup chopped green sweet pepper

½ cup chopped carrot

2 cloves garlic, minced

2 cups chopped, peeled potatoes

1 cup reduced-sodium chicken broth

1 bay leaf

1 sprig fresh thyme

¼ tsp. crushed red pepper

1 14.5-oz. can diced tomatoes, undrained

1. Chop shucked clams, reserving juice. Strain clam juice to remove bits of shell. (Or drain canned clams, reserving juice.) If necessary, add water to reserved juice to equal 1½ cups.

2. In a 4-qt. pot cook bacon over medium heat until crisp. Drain bacon on paper towels, reserving drippings in pot. Add the next five ingredients (through garlic) to the reserved drippings. Cook 5 minutes or until tender, stirring occasionally.

3. Stir in reserved clam juice and the next five ingredients (through crushed red pepper). Bring to boiling; reduce heat. Simmer, covered, 10 to 15 minutes or until potatoes are tender.

4. Stir in tomatoes and the clams. Return to boiling; reduce heat. Cook 1 minute. Discard bay leaf and thyme sprig. Sprinkle servings with the bacon.

PER SERVING: 372 cal., 16 g fat (5 g sat. fat), 59 mg chol., 1,373 mg sodium, 31 g carb., 5 g fiber, 7 g sugars, 26 g pro.

FAST PREP

new england clam chowder

START TO FINISH: 30 minutes | **MAKES:** 6 servings (1 cup each)

1 pint shucked clams or two 6.5-oz. cans minced clams, undrained

1 8-oz. bottle clam juice

3 slices bacon, chopped

1 cup chopped onion

½ cup chopped celery

3 cups chopped, peeled potatoes

1 tsp. snipped fresh thyme

¼ tsp. black pepper

2 cups half-and-half

1. Chop fresh clams (if using), reserving juice; set clams aside. Strain fresh clam juice to remove bits of shell. (Or drain canned clams, reserving juice.) Add enough of the bottled clam juice to the reserved clam juice to measure 2 cups.

2. In a 3-qt. pot cook bacon over medium heat until crisp. Drain bacon on paper towels, reserving 1 Tbsp. drippings in pot. Add onion and celery to the reserved drippings. Cook 5 minutes or until soft, stirring occasionally.

3. Add the 2 cups clam juice, the potatoes, thyme, and pepper. Bring to boiling; reduce heat. Simmer 10 to 15 minutes or until potatoes are tender. Using a slotted spoon, remove 1 cup of potatoes; set aside. Using a handheld immersion blender, blend soup until smooth (see tip, *below*).

4. Add clams and the reserved potatoes to soup. Return to boiling; reduce heat and cook 1 minute. Stir in half-and-half; heat through. Sprinkle servings with bacon and, if desired, additional thyme.

PER SERVING: *278 cal., 14 g fat (7 g sat. fat), 58 mg chol., 633 mg sodium, 22 g carb., 2 g fiber, 5 g sugars, 17 g pro.*

NO IMMERSION BLENDER?

You can puree the soup mixture in a blender instead. Let the soup cool slightly, then blend the soup, about one-fourth at a time, holding a folded kitchen towel firmly over the lid (this will prevent steam from blowing the lid off the blender when you turn it on). Return all the pureed mixture to the pot and continue with the soup as directed.

pacific salmon chowder

START TO FINISH: 50 minutes | **MAKES:** 6 servings (1½ cups each)

1 lb. fresh or frozen skinless salmon fillets (tip, *right*)

1 Tbsp. butter

½ cup chopped fennel (reserve fronds)

2 cloves garlic, minced

1 32-oz. box reduced-sodium chicken or vegetable broth

1¼ lb. Yukon gold potatoes, peeled (if desired) and cut into ½-inch pieces

½ tsp. salt

¼ tsp. black pepper

1½ cups half-and-half

2 Tbsp. all-purpose flour

1 tsp. lemon zest

1. Thaw salmon, if frozen. Rinse salmon; pat dry with paper towels. Cut into 1-inch pieces.

2. In a 4-qt. pot melt butter over medium heat. Add chopped fennel; cook 5 to 6 minutes or until tender, stirring occasionally. Add garlic; cook and stir 1 minute more.

3. Add the next four ingredients (through pepper). Bring to boiling; reduce heat. Simmer, uncovered, 10 minutes or until potatoes are tender.

4. In a bowl combine 1 cup of the half-and-half and the flour; stir into soup. Cook and stir until slightly thickened and bubbly. Stir in salmon. Return just to boiling; reduce heat. Simmer gently, uncovered, 3 to 5 minutes or until salmon flakes easily. Stir in the remaining ½ cup half-and-half; heat through. Stir in lemon zest. Top servings with fennel fronds.

PER SERVING: 286 cal., 14 g fat (6 g sat. fat), 69 mg chol., 651 mg sodium, 20 g carb., 2 g fiber, 4 g sugars, 21 g pro.

ALL ABOUT SALMON

The rich and fatty (good fat, of course!) flesh of salmon is a regular rotation on dinner tables across America. And because it contains healthful omega-3s, it can be consumed without guilt a couple times a week. There are many varieties of salmon on the market, and much of what is available is farmed. If offered the choice, go for wild-caught salmon. The flavor is often deeper and richer.

southern ham and sweet potato chowder

PREP: 20 minutes | **COOK:** 15 minutes | **MAKES:** 6 to 8 servings (1⅓ cups each)

2 Tbsp. butter

1 cup chopped onion

1 cup chopped celery

½ cup chopped carrot

4 cups reduced-sodium chicken broth

2 cups chopped, peeled sweet potatoes

1 cup half-and-half

3 Tbsp. all-purpose flour

2 cups cubed cooked reduced-sodium ham

2 cups shredded white cheddar cheese (8 oz.)

¼ cup sliced green onions (optional)

1. In a 6-qt. pot melt butter over medium heat. Add onion, celery, and carrot; cook about 7 minutes or until vegetables are soft, stirring occasionally. Add broth and sweet potatoes. Bring to boiling; reduce heat. Simmer, uncovered, 8 to 10 minutes or until sweet potatoes are tender.

2. In a bowl whisk together half-and-half and flour; add flour mixture and ham to soup. Cook and stir until slightly thickened and bubbly. Cook and stir 1 minute more. Gradually add cheese, stirring until melted and smooth. If desired, top servings with green onions.

PER SERVING: *361 cal., 23 g fat (14 g sat. fat), 84 mg chol., 1,027 mg sodium, 19 g carb., 2 g fiber, 6 g sugars, 22 g pro.*

Cincinnati Chili, *page 199*

chili time

When cooler weather hits, it's prime time for a big pot of chili. Turn up the heat with red, white, or green chili, customize the toppers, and settle in for some heartwarming comfort.

| FAST PREP

beefy texas chili

PREP: 30 minutes | **COOK:** 2 hours 5 minutes | **MAKES:** 4 to 6 servings (1⅔ cups each)

3 Tbsp. vegetable oil

2½ to 3 lb. boneless beef chuck pot roast, trimmed of fat and cut into ½-inch cubes*

Black pepper

1½ cups chopped onions

4 cloves garlic, minced

1 Tbsp. ground cumin

1½ to 2 tsp. ground ancho chile pepper

4 cups reduced-sodium beef broth

1 14.5-oz. can diced tomatoes, undrained

1 8-oz. can tomato sauce

1 to 2 canned chipotle peppers in adobo sauce, finely chopped (tip, *page 14*)

3 Tbsp. very finely crushed tortilla chips or masa harina

Toppings such as sour cream, snipped fresh cilantro, sliced fresh jalapeño chile peppers (tip, *page 14*), and/or shredded cheddar cheese

1. In a 4- to 5-qt. pot heat 1 Tbsp. of the oil over medium-high heat. Sprinkle meat with black pepper. Add one-third of the meat to the pot; cook until browned. Remove meat from pot, draining off liquid. Repeat twice with remaining oil and meat.

2. Add onions and garlic to the pot (add additional oil if needed). Cook and stir 4 minutes or until tender. Add cumin and ancho pepper; cook and stir 1 minute more.

3. Return meat to pot. Add the next four ingredients (through chipotle peppers). Bring to boiling over medium-high heat; reduce heat to low. Simmer, covered, 1 hour, stirring occasionally. Uncover and simmer 1 hour more or until beef is tender and chili is slightly thickened, stirring occasionally.

4. Slowly add crushed chips to the chili, stirring constantly to incorporate. Simmer 5 minutes. Serve with toppings.

*TIP: If you prefer, use ground beef chuck instead of the roast.

PER SERVING: 667 cal., 29 g fat (8 g sat. fat), 198 mg chol., 1,433 mg sodium, 30 g carb., 6 g fiber, 14 g sugars, 72 g pro.

AS MANY TEXANS WILL TELL YOU, AUTHENTIC "BOWL OF RED" CHILI DOES NOT INCLUDE BEANS. HOWEVER, YOU MAY ADD ONE CAN OF BEANS OF YOUR CHOICE, DRAINED AND RINSED, IF YOU PREFER.

Roasted

Turkey Chili

Three Bean

| FAST PREP

traditional chili + 6 to try

PREP: 25 minutes | COOK: 20 minutes | MAKES: 8 servings (1¼ cups each)

1½ lb. lean ground beef

3 cups chopped carrots, celery, onions, and/or sweet peppers

4 cloves garlic, minced

1 Tbsp. vegetable oil

2 15-oz. cans black beans and/ or kidney beans, rinsed and drained

2 14.5-oz. cans diced tomatoes, undrained

1 15-oz. can tomato sauce

1 cup reduced-sodium beef broth

2 Tbsp. chili powder

1 tsp. dried oregano, crushed

½ tsp. black pepper or crushed red pepper

Desired toppings, such as cheese, sour cream, snipped cilantro, and/or sliced avocado

1. In a 6-qt. pot cook ground beef, chopped vegetables, and garlic in hot oil over medium-high heat until meat is browned and vegetables are tender. Drain off fat.

2. Stir the next seven ingredients (through pepper) into meat mixture. Bring to boiling over medium-high heat; reduce heat to low. Simmer, covered, 20 minutes, stirring occasionally. Serve with desired toppings.

PER SERVING: 303 cal., 11 g fat (4 g sat. fat), 55 mg chol., 929 mg sodium, 28 g carb., 9 g fiber, 7 g sugars, 25 g pro.

BBQ PORK: Substitute 1½ lb. pork shoulder, trimmed of fat and cut into ¾-inch pieces, for the ground beef. Reduce tomato sauce to one 8-oz. can and add 1 cup barbecue sauce. Simmer 1½ hours.

THREE BEAN: Use three 15-oz. cans of a combination of black, pinto, garbanzo, and/or red beans in place of the 2 cans black beans.

TURKEY CHILI: Substitute ground turkey for the beef and cannellini beans for the black beans. Omit tomatoes, tomato sauce, beef broth, and chili powder. Add one 32-oz. box chicken broth, one 8-oz. jar salsa verde, and one 4-oz. can diced green chiles, undrained. Use cumin in place of the oregano.

ROASTED: Use chuck roast, trimmed of fat and cut into ¾-inch pieces, in place of the ground beef. Substitute fire-roasted diced tomatoes for the regular canned tomatoes and add ½ cup chopped roasted red sweet peppers and ½ tsp. smoked paprika. Simmer 1½ hours.

MEXICAN: Use 1½ cups chopped, seeded poblano peppers and ½ cup chopped onion in place of the 3 cups vegetables. Add 1 tsp. ground cumin and 2 chipotle chiles in adobo sauce, finely chopped (tip, *page 14*), with the oregano. Stir in ⅓ cup snipped fresh cilantro and ¼ cup lime juice before serving. Serve with lime wedges.

SURF AND TURF: Use 1 lb. thinly sliced boneless top sirloin plus 8 oz. sliced fully cooked andouille sausage in place of the ground beef and substitute Cajun seasoning for the oregano. Simmer, covered, 20 minutes. Add 12 oz. peeled and deveined shrimp; simmer 5 minutes more.

southwestern meatball chili

START TO FINISH: 25 minutes | **MAKES:** 4 servings (1 cup each)

1   14- to 16-oz. pkg. fully cooked refrigerated or frozen beef meatballs (thawed if frozen)

1   16-oz. pkg. Santa Fe medley frozen mixed vegetables (corn, black beans, and red sweet peppers)

2   cups chopped fresh tomatoes and/or cherry tomatoes

1½ cups water

3   Tbsp. tomato paste

1   Tbsp. chili powder

Sliced jalapeño chile peppers (tip, *page 14*), halved cherry tomatoes, and/or fresh cilantro (optional)

1. In a 4-qt. pot combine the first six ingredients (through chili powder). Cover and cook over medium-low heat 20 minutes, stirring occasionally. If desired, top servings with jalapeño peppers, cherry tomatoes, and/or cilantro.

PER SERVING: 386 cal., 24 g fat (11 g sat. fat), 93 mg chol., 944 mg sodium, 25 g carb., 8 g fiber, 9 g sugars, 20 g pro.

ITALIAN MEATBALL CHILI: Prepare as directed, except substitute turkey meatballs for the beef meatballs; one 16-oz. pkg. frozen carrots, peas, and green beans for the Santa Fe vegetables; and 1 Tbsp. dried Italian seasoning, crushed, for the chili powder.

cincinnati chili pictured on page 192

PREP: 30 minutes | **COOK:** 30 minutes | **MAKES:** 6 servings (1⅓ cups each)

2 lb. ground beef chuck

2 cups chopped onions

2 Tbsp. chili powder

¾ tsp. ground cumin

¾ tsp. ground cinnamon

½ tsp. salt

¼ tsp. cayenne pepper

4 cloves garlic, minced

1½ cups water

1 15- to 16-oz. can dark red kidney beans, rinsed and drained

1 15-oz. can tomato sauce

1 tsp. Worcestershire sauce

½ oz. unsweetened chocolate, chopped (optional)

Hot cooked spaghetti or crusty bread

Shredded cheddar cheese

1. In a 4- to 6-qt. pot cook beef and onions over medium heat until meat is browned. Drain off fat. Add the next six ingredients (through garlic). Cook and stir 1 to 2 minutes more or until fragrant.

2. Add the water, beans, tomato sauce, and Worcestershire sauce to meat mixture in pot. Bring to boiling over medium-high heat; reduce heat to low. Simmer, uncovered, 30 minutes, stirring occasionally. If desired, stir in chocolate until melted.

3. Serve chili over hot cooked spaghetti and sprinkle with cheese.

PER SERVING: *590 cal., 31 g fat (12 g sat. fat), 111 mg chol., 848 mg sodium, 41 g carb., 6 g fiber, 6 g sugars, 36 g pro.*

 FAST PREP

pork and poblano chili

PREP: 25 minutes | **SLOW COOK:** 7 to 8 hours (low) or 3½ to 4 hours (high)
MAKES: 6 to 8 servings (1½ cups each)

2	fresh poblano chile peppers, halved and seeded (tip, *page 14*)
1	green sweet pepper, halved and seeded
3	cloves garlic
1½	lb. lean ground pork
1	cup chopped onion
2	15-oz. cans Great Northern beans, rinsed and drained
1	16-oz. jar mild or medium green salsa
1	14.5-oz. can chicken broth
1½	tsp. ground cumin
¼	cup snipped fresh cilantro
	Corn chips or baked tortilla strips* (optional)
	Sour cream (optional)

1. In a food processor combine poblano peppers, sweet pepper, and garlic. Cover and process until finely chopped; set aside. In a large skillet cook pork and onion over medium heat until meat is browned and onion is tender. Drain off fat. Add pepper mixture; cook and stir 2 to 3 minutes more or until peppers are tender.

2. In a 3½- or 4-qt. slow cooker combine meat mixture and the next four ingredients (through cumin).

3. Cover and cook on low 7 to 8 hours or on high 3½ to 4 hours; cool slightly. If desired, mash beans slightly with a potato masher.

4. Before serving, stir in cilantro. If desired, serve with corn chips and sour cream.

PER SERVING: *430 cal., 19 g fat (7 g sat. fat), 74 mg chol., 1,152 mg sodium, 37 g carb., 9 g fiber, 4 g sugars, 27 g pro.*

*TIP: For baked tortilla strips, preheat oven to 350°F. Brush flour tortillas with vegetable oil and sprinkle with chili powder. Cut tortillas into ½-inch strips. Place in a single layer on a baking sheet and bake 5 to 10 minutes or until golden and crisp; cool.

chili verde

PREP: 25 minutes | **SLOW COOK:** 6 to 7 hours (low) or 3½ to 4 hours (high) | **MAKES:** 6 servings (1½ cups each)

1 Tbsp. olive oil

1 1½-lb. boneless pork shoulder roast, trimmed of fat and cut into ¾-inch pieces

1 15-oz. can Great Northern or navy beans, rinsed and drained

12 oz. fresh tomatillos, husked and chopped, or two 11-oz. cans tomatillos, rinsed, drained, and coarsely chopped

½ cup chopped onion

1 4-oz. can diced green chile peppers, undrained

2 cloves garlic, minced

¾ tsp. ground cumin

½ tsp. salt

1 14.5-oz. can chicken broth

1 cup chopped fresh spinach

2 tsp. lime juice

Sour cream (optional)

Snipped fresh cilantro (optional)

1. In a large skillet heat oil over medium-high heat. Cook meat, half at a time, in the hot oil until browned. Drain off fat.

2. Place meat in a 3½- or 4-qt. slow cooker. Stir in the next seven ingredients (through salt). Pour broth over meat mixture in cooker.

3. Cover and cook on low 6 to 7 hours or on high 3½ to 4 hours.

4. Stir in spinach and lime juice. If desired, top servings with sour cream and/or cilantro.

PER SERVING: 300 cal., 11 g fat (3 g sat. fat), 76 mg chol., 606 mg sodium, 21 g carb., 4 g fiber, 0 g sugars, 29 g pro.

FOR 8 SERVINGS: Use a 5- to 6-qt. slow cooker. Increase the meat to 2 lb. and brown in an extra-large skillet. Use two 15-oz. cans Great Northern beans or navy beans, 1¼ lb. fresh tomatillos or three 11-oz. cans tomatillos, ¾ cup chopped onion, 3 cloves garlic, 1 tsp. ground cumin, two 14.5-oz. cans chicken broth, 2 cups chopped fresh spinach, and 1 Tbsp. lime juice. (Do not change the amounts of olive oil, green chile peppers, and salt.)

harvest chicken lentil chili

PREP: 40 minutes | **COOK:** 30 minutes | **MAKES:** 8 servings (1⅓ cups each)

2 Tbsp. olive oil

1 cup coarsely chopped onion

1 cup coarsely chopped carrots

1 cup chopped celery

2 lb. skinless, boneless chicken thighs or breasts, cut into bite-size pieces*

4 cups reduced-sodium chicken broth

1 15-oz. can pumpkin

1 14.5-oz. can diced tomatoes, undrained

¾ cup dried brown lentils, rinsed and drained

4 tsp. chili powder

1 tsp. dried oregano, crushed

   Salt and black pepper

   Plain fat-free Greek yogurt, roasted pumpkin seeds (pepitas), and/or chili powder (optional)

1. In a 4- to 5-qt. pot heat 1 Tbsp. of the oil over medium-high heat. Add onion, carrots, and celery. Cook and stir until vegetables begin to soften. Remove from pot. Add the remaining 1 Tbsp. oil. Brown chicken, half at a time, in the hot oil.

2. Return all the chicken to the pot. Add the next six ingredients (through oregano). Bring to boiling over medium-high heat; reduce heat to low. Simmer, covered, 30 to 40 minutes or until lentils are tender, stirring occasionally. Season to taste with salt and pepper. If desired, serve with yogurt, pumpkin seeds, and/or additional chili powder.

PER SERVING: *286 cal., 8 g fat (2 g sat. fat), 106 mg chol., 558 mg sodium, 23 g carb., 6 g fiber, 6 g sugars, 30 g pro.*

*TIP: If desired, use 2 lb. ground chicken or ground turkey in place of the cut-up chicken.

chipotle turkey chili

PREP: 25 minutes | **COOK:** 30 minutes | **MAKES:** 8 servings (1¼ cups each)

1 Tbsp. vegetable oil

2 lb. boneless turkey breast tenderloin, cut into small pieces

1½ cups chopped sweet onions

3 poblano and/or Anaheim chile peppers, seeded and chopped (tip, *page 14*)

½ tsp. kosher salt

1 15-oz. can tomato sauce

1 14.5-oz. can diced tomatoes, undrained

1 14.5-oz. can reduced-sodium chicken broth

1 cup dried lentils, rinsed and drained

1 Tbsp. finely chopped chipotle chile pepper in adobo sauce (tip, *page 14*)

1 Tbsp. chili powder

Sour cream and sliced jalapeño chile peppers (tip, *page 14*) (optional)

1. In a 5- to 6- qt. pot heat oil over medium-high heat. Add turkey and cook until browned. Remove turkey from pot. Add onions, chile peppers, and salt; cook and stir 3 minutes.

2. Return turkey to pot. Add the next six ingredients (through chili powder). Bring to boiling over medium-high heat; reduce heat to low. Simmer, covered, 30 minutes or until lentils are tender, stirring occasionally. If desired, serve with sour cream, jalapeño peppers, and additional chili powder.

PER SERVING: 277 cal., 4 g fat (1 g sat. fat), 65 mg chol., 655 mg sodium, 25 g carb., 10 g fiber, 7 g sugars, 35 g pro.

white chicken chili

PREP: 25 minutes | **SLOW COOK:** 8 to 10 hours (low) or 4 to 5 hours (high) | **MAKES:** 6 servings (1⅔ cups each)

3 15- to 16-oz. cans Great Northern, pinto, or cannellini (white kidney) beans, rinsed and drained

2½ cups chopped cooked chicken*

1½ cups chopped red, green, and/or yellow sweet peppers

1 cup chopped onion

2 jalapeño chile peppers, seeded and chopped (tip, *page 14*)

2 tsp. ground cumin

2 cloves garlic, minced

½ tsp. salt

½ tsp. dried oregano, crushed

3½ cups chicken broth

Shredded Monterey Jack cheese (optional)

Broken tortilla chips (optional)

1. In a 3½- or 4-qt. slow cooker stir together the first nine ingredients (through oregano). Add broth. Cover and cook on low 8 to 10 hours or on high 4 to 5 hours. If desired, top with cheese and tortilla chips.

PER SERVING: *422 cal., 6 g fat (2 g sat. fat), 52 mg chol., 709 mg sodium, 54 g carb., 13 g fiber, 1 g sugars, 38 g pro.*

*TIP: For cooked chicken, use meat from a deli rotisserie chicken or use leftover cooked chicken. You also may purchase packages of refrigerated or frozen precooked chicken.

chicken fajita chili

PREP: 25 minutes | **SLOW COOK:** 4 to 5 hours (low) or 2 to 2½ hours (high) | **MAKES:** 6 servings (1½ cups each)

1 Tbsp. chili powder

1 tsp. fajita seasoning

½ tsp. ground cumin

2 cloves garlic, minced

2 lb. skinless, boneless chicken breast halves, cut into 1-inch pieces

Nonstick cooking spray

2 14.5-oz. cans no-salt-added diced tomatoes, undrained

1 19-oz. can cannellini beans (white kidney beans), rinsed and drained

1 16-oz. pkg. frozen (yellow, green, and red) sweet peppers and onion stir-fry vegetables

3 Tbsp. shredded reduced-fat cheddar cheese (optional)

3 Tbsp. light sour cream (optional)

3 Tbsp. purchased guacamole (optional)

1. In a medium bowl stir together the first four ingredients (through garlic). Add chicken; gently toss to coat chicken. Coat a large skillet with cooking spray; heat skillet over medium-high heat. Cook half of the chicken in hot skillet until browned, stirring occasionally. Place cooked chicken in a 3½- or 4-qt. slow cooker. Repeat with the remaining chicken.

2. Add tomatoes, beans, and frozen vegetables to chicken in slow cooker; stir to combine.

3. Cover and cook on low 4 to 5 hours or on high 2 to 2½ hours. If desired, serve with cheese, sour cream, and guacamole.

PER SERVING: 261 cal., 2 g fat (1 g sat. fat), 88 mg chol., 294 mg sodium, 22 g carb., 7 g fiber, 7 g sugars, 41 g pro.

Cuban Beef Sandwich, *page 223*

under
pressure

Welcome the modern pressure cooker to your home. This appliance cuts down cooking time while yielding moist, tender meals. No pressure cooker? No problem. Each recipe has slow cooker directions, too!

pressure cooking 101

ELECTRIC The electric models look like slow cookers (and often have that function). Once you read the directions, they are easy to set—just hit a button or two. They require no further supervision and have a timer that tracks how long it takes the cooker to get up to pressure, cook the food, and depressurize.

Ease of use
Overall, these are very easy and convenient to use.

Versatility
Most cookers have multiple settings, such as brown, pressure cook, slow cook, rice, keep warm, and more.

Price
Prices hover around $100 but can be higher or lower, depending on models.

USING AN ELECTRIC PRESSURE COOKER

All models differ in appearance, parts, and instructions (read your user's manual before you start!), but here's the gist of pressure cooking.

1. CHECK IT OFF Take a quick look at all the parts of your pressure cooker. Make sure the gasket is soft, flexible, and crack-free. Snap it into place as directed in the manual. Make sure the pressure valve is free of debris and in place.

2. BROWNING = FLAVOR Most models have a browning function, which is essential if you want your meats to have rich, caramelized flavor. Add oil, set the browning function, and allow the pot to heat up. Meat should be browned in batches to prevent the pot from cooling down and steaming the meat instead of browning it.

3. EVERYTHING IN! Once the meat is browned, add the remaining ingredients or as directed in your recipe. Lock the lid into place and adjust the pressure

How does it work? When any food cooks, it produces steam. The pressure cooker has an airtight seal (thanks to the gasket under the lid), so steam is trapped and creates intense pressure inside the cooker (and therefore much higher heat). These intense cooking conditions cook food more quickly and more evenly than any other method. Here are the two main types of pressure cookers.

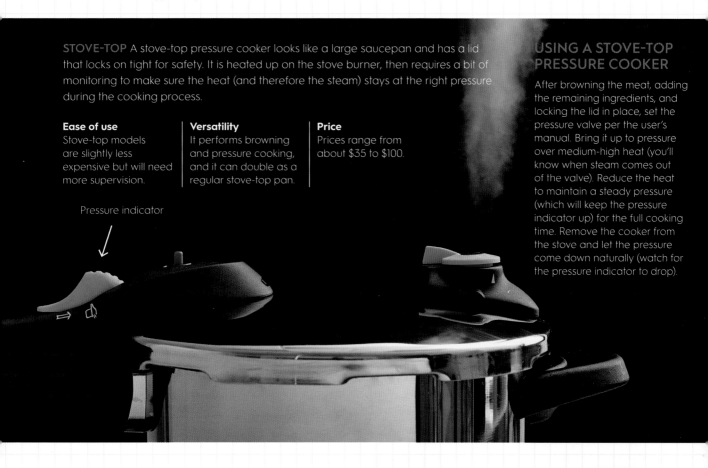

STOVE-TOP A stove-top pressure cooker looks like a large saucepan and has a lid that locks on tight for safety. It is heated up on the stove burner, then requires a bit of monitoring to make sure the heat (and therefore the steam) stays at the right pressure during the cooking process.

Ease of use
Stove-top models are slightly less expensive but will need more supervision.

Versatility
It performs browning and pressure cooking, and it can double as a regular stove-top pan.

Price
Prices range from about $35 to $100.

Pressure indicator

USING A STOVE-TOP PRESSURE COOKER

After browning the meat, adding the remaining ingredients, and locking the lid in place, set the pressure valve per the user's manual. Bring it up to pressure over medium-high heat (you'll know when steam comes out of the valve). Reduce the heat to maintain a steady pressure (which will keep the pressure indicator up) for the full cooking time. Remove the cooker from the stove and let the pressure come down naturally (watch for the pressure indicator to drop).

valve to the closed position. Select the setting and time. The digital display will indicate when the cooker has gotten up to pressure (this usually takes about 15 or 20 minutes) and the actual cooking time has started to count down.

4. LETTING OFF STEAM When the cooking time is done, the cooker will automatically begin to depressurize, which is called "natural release." This takes about 15 minutes (quick release happens when you open the pressure valve and let the steam rush out—which isn't recommended for liquid

recipes, such as soup). When the pressure has dropped, the pressure indicator will sink down and you will be able to open the lid. (Until then, the lid stays locked.) After 15 minutes of depressurizing, if the lid is still locked, you can often open the pressure valve to let out any remaining steam.

5. OPEN SESAME! Now for the fun part—seeing what's inside! The food

is still extremely hot, so steam will come out when you open the lid. Be careful—watch your arms and face so you don't get burned.

6. CLEANING UP After cooking, clean the removable parts in hot, soapy water, including the pot liner, lid, steam catcher, gasket, and any removable parts on the lid as described in your user's manual.

beer-soaked brisket sandwiches

PREP: 30 minutes | **PRESSURE COOK:** 1½ hours + time to build pressure | **MAKES:** 10 servings (1 sandwich each)

1 3½- to 4-lb. beef brisket (flat half), fat trimmed to ¼-inch thickness

½ tsp. salt

½ tsp. black pepper

1 Tbsp. vegetable oil

1 12-oz. bottle wheat beer

1 medium onion, sliced

4 cloves garlic, smashed and peeled

¼ cup Dijon-style mustard

1 Tbsp. hoisin sauce

¼ tsp. ground cloves

1 1-lb. loaf rectangular ciabatta bread, split, toasted, and cut into 3-inch pieces

2 medium carrots, peeled and cut into ribbons

Napa cabbage

Fresh parsley (optional)

1. Use a 6-qt. electric or stove-top pressure cooker. Sprinkle brisket with salt and pepper. For an electric pressure cooker, use the sauté setting to brown meat, half at a time, in hot oil. For a stove-top cooker, brown meat, half at a time, in hot oil in the cooker. Remove beef; drain off fat.

2. Add beer, onion, and garlic to cooker. Stir to scrape up any browned bits from bottom of pan. In a bowl whisk together mustard, hoisin, and cloves. Spread over top of brisket. Place brisket in cooker on top of onion mixture. Lock lid in place.

3. Set electric cooker on high pressure to cook 1½ hours. For stove-top cooker, bring up to pressure over medium-high heat according to manufacturer's directions; reduce heat enough to maintain steady (but not excessive) pressure according to manufacturer's directions. Cook 1½ hours. Remove from heat. Quickly release the pressure according to manufacturer's directions. Open lid carefully.

4. Transfer meat to a platter; cover to keep warm. Skim fat from cooking liquid. Strain through a fine-mesh sieve lined with a double layer of 100%-cotton cheesecloth. Season with additional salt and pepper. To serve, slice beef across the grain. Top bread with beef, carrots, and cabbage. If desired, garnish with parsley. Serve with cooking liquid.

SLOW COOKER DIRECTIONS: Sprinkle brisket with salt and pepper. In an extra-large skillet brown meat, half at a time, in hot oil over medium-high heat. Place beer, onion, and garlic in a 6-qt. slow cooker; top with brisket. In a bowl whisk together mustard, hoisin, and cloves. Spread over top of brisket. Cover and cook on low 10 to 12 hours or high 5 to 6 hours. Transfer meat to a platter and continue as directed in Step 4.

PER SERVING: 427 cal., 17 g fat (6 g sat. fat), 106 mg chol., 559 mg sodium, 28 g carb., 2 g fiber, 3 g sugars, 37 g pro.

| FAST PREP

cuban beef sandwich

PREP: 20 minutes | **PRESSURE COOK:** 30 minutes + time to build pressure | **STAND:** 15 minutes | **MAKES:** 6 servings (1 sandwich each)

- 1 tsp. dried oregano, crushed
- 1 tsp. ground cumin
- ½ tsp. salt
- ½ tsp. black pepper
- ⅛ tsp. ground allspice
- 1 2- to 2½-lb. boneless beef chuck roast, trimmed of fat and cut into 2-inch pieces
- 1 Tbsp. vegetable oil
- 2 medium onions, sliced
- 1 large green sweet pepper, sliced
- 4 cloves garlic, minced
- ¼ cup orange juice
- ¼ cup lime juice
- 1 avocado, halved, seeded, peeled, and sliced
  Citrus Mayo
- 6 bolillo or hoagie rolls, split and toasted

1. Use a 4- to 6-qt. stove-top or electric pressure cooker. In a small bowl combine the first five ingredients (through allspice). Rub spice mixture onto all sides of the beef pieces.

2. In a stove-top pressure cooker cook meat in hot oil over medium-high heat until browned. (For an electric pressure cooker, use the sauté setting to brown meat in hot oil.) Remove meat from cooker. Place onions, sweet pepper, and garlic in cooker. Add orange juice and lime juice. Place meat on top of vegetables. Lock lid in place. Set electric cooker on high pressure to cook 30 minutes. For stove-top cooker, bring up to pressure over medium-high heat according to manufacturer's directions; reduce heat enough to maintain steady (but not excessive) pressure according to manufacturer's directions. Cook 30 minutes. Remove from heat. For electric and stove-top models, let stand to release pressure naturally at least 15 minutes. If necessary, carefully open steam vent to release any remaining pressure. Open lid carefully.

3. Remove meat from pressure cooker. Shred meat using two forks; place shredded meat in a large bowl. Strain cooking liquid, reserving vegetables. Add ¼ to ½ cup cooking liquid to meat to moisten. Stir in reserved vegetables. (Discard remaining cooking liquid.) Serve on rolls with Citrus Mayo and avocado.

CITRUS MAYO: In a small bowl whisk together ¼ cup reduced-fat mayonnaise, ½ tsp. orange zest, 1 tsp. orange juice, ¼ tsp. lime zest and ½ tsp. lime juice, ⅛ tsp. salt, and a pinch black pepper.

SLOW COOKER DIRECTIONS: Prepare meat as directed in Step 1. In a large skillet cook meat, half at a time, in hot oil over medium-high heat until browned. In a 4- to 6-qt. slow cooker layer onions, sweet pepper, and garlic. Pour orange juice and lime juice over vegetables. Place meat on vegetables. Cover; cook on low 8 hours or on high 4 hours. Remove meat from slow cooker. Continue as directed in Step 3.

PER SERVING: 383 cal., 12 g fat (3 g sat. fat), 64 mg chol., 702 mg sodium, 40 g carb., 4 g fiber, 4 g sugars, 28 g pro.

short rib goulash

PREP: 30 minutes | **PRESSURE COOK:** 30 minutes + time to build pressure | **STAND:** 15 minutes
MAKES: 8 servings (1 short rib + ½ cup squash + ¼ cup sauce each)

8 bone-in beef short ribs (3¾ to 4½ lb. total), trimmed of fat

1 Tbsp. paprika

2 tsp. kosher salt

¼ tsp. freshly ground black pepper

2 Tbsp. olive oil

2 lb. butternut squash and/or rutabaga, peeled, seeded, and cut into 2-inch cubes (about 4 cups)

½ cup reduced-sodium beef broth

½ cup dry red wine

2 Tbsp. soy sauce

4 cloves garlic, minced

1 tsp. dried thyme, crushed

2 Tbsp. tomato paste

2 Tbsp. prepared horseradish

Hot cooked noodles

Fresh thyme

1. Use a 6-qt. electric or stove-top pressure cooker. Sprinkle ribs with paprika, salt, and pepper. For an electric cooker, use the sauté setting to brown ribs, half at a time, in hot oil. For a stove-top cooker, brown meat, half at a time, in hot oil in cooker. Return all meat to cooker. Add the next six ingredients (through dried thyme). Lock lid in place.

2. Set electric cooker on high pressure to cook 30 minutes. For stove-top cooker, bring up to pressure over medium-high heat according to manufacturer's directions; reduce heat enough to maintain steady (but not excessive) pressure according to manufacturer's directions. Cook 30 minutes. Remove from heat. Let stand to release pressure naturally at least 15 minutes or according to manufacturer's directions. If necessary, carefully open steam vent to release any remaining pressure. Open lid carefully.

3. Transfer ribs and vegetables to a serving dish. Skim fat from cooking liquid. Whisk in tomato paste and horseradish. Serve sauce with ribs and noodles. Top with fresh thyme.

SLOW COOKER DIRECTIONS: Sprinkle ribs with paprika, salt, and pepper. In a very large skillet cook meat in hot oil over medium-high heat until well browned, turning occasionally. Place meat in a 6-qt. slow cooker. Add the next six ingredients (through dried thyme). Cover and cook on low 10 to 12 hours or on high 5 to 6 hours. Transfer ribs and vegetables to a serving dish. Skim fat from cooking liquid. Whisk in tomato paste and horseradish. Serve as directed.

PER SERVING: *684 cal., 43 g fat (18 g sat. fat), 159 mg chol., 773 mg sodium, 30 g carb., 3 g fiber, 4 g sugars, 42 g pro.*

old-fashioned beef stew

PREP: 20 minutes | **PRESSURE COOK:** 12 minutes + time to build pressure | **STAND:** 15 minutes
MAKES: 6 servings (2 cups each)

¼ cup all-purpose flour

½ tsp. salt

¼ tsp. black pepper

2 lb. beef chuck roast or beef stew meat, trimmed of fat and cut into 1-inch pieces

3 Tbsp. vegetable oil

2 medium onions, cut into thin wedges

1 cup thinly sliced celery

4 red-skin potatoes, cut into 1-inch cubes

4 carrots, bias-sliced ¼ inch thick

3 cups vegetable juice

3 cups reduced-sodium beef broth

2 Tbsp. Worcestershire sauce

1 tsp. dried oregano or thyme, crushed

1. Use a 6-qt. stove-top or electric pressure cooker. In a large plastic bag combine flour, salt, and pepper. Add meat to bag; shake until evenly coated. In a stove-top pressure cooker heat half of the oil over medium-high heat; add half of the meat and cook until browned. (For an electric pressure cooker, use the sauté setting to brown meat in the oil.) Remove meat from cooker. Repeat with remaining meat and oil.

2. Return all meat to pressure cooker. Add the remaining ingredients. Lock lid in place. Set electric cooker on high pressure to cook 12 minutes. For stove-top cooker, bring up to pressure over medium-high heat according to manufacturer's directions; reduce heat enough to maintain steady (but not excessive) pressure according to manufacturer's directions. Cook 12 minutes. Remove from heat. For electric and stove-top models, let stand to release pressure naturally at least 15 minutes or according to manufacturer's directions. If necessary, carefully open steam vent to release any remaining pressure. Open lid carefully. Season to taste with additional salt and pepper.

SLOW COOKER DIRECTIONS: Coat meat with flour mixture as directed. In a large pot brown half of the meat in half of the oil over medium-high heat; remove meat. Repeat with remaining meat and oil. In a 4- to 6-qt. slow cooker layer meat, onions, celery, potatoes, and carrots. Decrease vegetable juice to 2 cups. Combine vegetable juice, broth, Worcestershire sauce, and oregano. Pour over meat and vegetables in slow cooker. Cover and cook on low 10 to 12 hours or on high 5 to 6 hours or until meat and vegetables are tender. Season to taste with additional salt and pepper.

PER SERVING: 413 cal., 13 g fat (3 g sat. fat), 98 mg chol., 831 mg sodium, 33 g carb., 5 g fiber, 10 g sugars, 39 g pro.

FAST PREP

pork stew with gremolata

PREP: 25 minutes | **PRESSURE COOK:** 8 or 10 minutes + time to build pressure | **STAND:** 15 minutes
MAKES: 4 servings (1¾ cups each)

1½   lb. boneless pork shoulder roast, trimmed of fat and cut into 1-inch pieces (tip, *opposite*)

1   Tbsp. olive oil

1   14.5-oz. can diced tomatoes, undrained

1   14.5-oz. can beef broth

1   large onion, cut into thin wedges

1   cup sliced carrots

½   cup sliced celery

½   cup dry white wine

2   cloves garlic, minced

½   tsp. dried thyme, crushed

¼   tsp. salt

⅛   tsp. black pepper

1   Tbsp. butter, softened

1   Tbsp. all-purpose flour

2   cups hot cooked orzo pasta or rice

   Gremolata

1. Use a 4- to 6-qt. stove-top or electric pressure cooker. In a stove-top pressure cooker cook meat, half at a time, in hot oil over medium-high heat until browned. (For an electric pressure cooker, use the sauté setting to brown meat in the hot oil.) Drain off fat. Stir in the next 10 ingredients (through pepper). Lock lid in place. Set electric cooker on high pressure to cook 10 minutes. For stove-top cooker, bring up to pressure over medium-high heat according to manufacturer's directions; reduce heat enough to maintain steady (but not excessive) pressure according to manufacturer's directions. Cook 8 minutes. Remove from heat. For electric and stove-top models, let stand to release pressure naturally at least 15 minutes or according to manufacturer's directions. If necessary, carefully open steam vent to release any remaining pressure. Open lid carefully.

2. In a small bowl combine butter and flour; whisk into stew. Cook over medium heat until slightly thickened and bubbly. Serve stew over hot cooked orzo and top with Gremolata.

SLOW COOKER DIRECTIONS: In a large skillet brown meat, half at a time, in hot oil over medium heat. Drain off fat. Transfer meat to a 3½- or 4-qt. slow cooker. Stir in the next 10 ingredients (through pepper) and 1 Tbsp. quick-cooking tapioca, crushed. Omit butter and flour. Cover and cook on low 7 to 8 hours or on high 3½ to 4 hours. Serve as directed.

PER SERVING: 480 cal., 16 g fat (6 g sat. fat), 109 mg chol., 936 mg sodium, 38 g carb, 5 g fiber, 7 g sugars, 39 g pro.

GREMOLATA: In a small bowl combine ¼ cup snipped fresh Italian parsley, 2 tsp. lemon zest, and 4 cloves garlic, minced.

CUT DOWN PREP TIME BY PURCHASING PRECUT PORK STEW MEAT FROM YOUR SUPERMARKET.

jamaican-style meat loaf

PREP: 25 minutes | **PRESSURE COOK:** 25 minutes + time to build pressure | **STAND:** 25 minutes | **MAKES:** 6 servings

1 lb. lean ground pork
1 lb. lean ground beef
1 cup shredded carrots
½ cup finely chopped onion
1 cup soft bread crumbs
2 eggs, lightly beaten
¼ cup strong brewed coffee
1 Tbsp. Worcestershire sauce
1 tsp. salt
¼ tsp. black pepper
1 cup beef broth or water
1 orange
Banana Topper (optional)
Fresh parsley (optional)

1. In a very large bowl combine the first 10 ingredients (through pepper). Mix well; shape into a round loaf. Cut three 18×3-inch heavy foil strips. Crisscross strips in the bottom of a 6-qt. electric or stove-top pressure cooker. Set loaf on strips. Add broth to cooker. Tuck ends of foil strips inside cooker. Lock lid in place.

2. Set electric cooker on high pressure to cook 25 minutes. For stove-top cooker, bring up to pressure over medium-high heat according to manufacturer's directions; reduce heat enough to maintain steady (but not excessive) pressure according to manufacturer's directions. Cook 25 minutes. Remove from heat. For electric and stove-top models, let stand to release pressure naturally at least 15 minutes. If necessary, carefully open steam vent to release any remaining pressure. Open lid. Use foil strips to lift meat from cooker, tilting to drain off fat. Transfer to a platter. Pull the foil strips from under meat. Cover; let stand 10 minutes. If desired, spoon Banana Topper over loaf and top with parsley.

SLOW COOKER DIRECTIONS: Mix and shape meat loaf as directed. Crisscross foil strips as directed in a 6-qt. oval or round slow cooker. Place meat loaf on strips; shape into an oval or round to match cooker shape, pressing loaf away from sides to prevent burning. Tuck ends of foil strips inside slow cooker. Cover; cook on low 5 hours or on high 2½ hours or until instant-read thermometer registers 165°F. Use foil strips to lift meat loaf from cooker, tilting to drain off fat. Transfer to a platter. Pull the foil strips from under meat loaf. Cover; let stand 10 minutes. Continue as directed.

PER SERVING: 458 cal., 27 g fat (9 g sat. fat), 168 mg chol., 738 mg sodium, 20 g carb., 3 g fiber, 11 g sugars, 33 g pro.

BANANA TOPPER: Melt 1 Tbsp. butter in skillet over medium-high heat. Add 1 medium banana, bias-sliced ½ inch thick; cook and stir 1 to 2 minutes or until caramelized. Remove banana from skillet. Add 1 Tbsp. vegetable oil to skillet. Add 6 miniature sweet peppers, seeded and sliced. Cook and stir 4 minutes. Add ⅓ cup coarsely chopped pitted green olives, 2 Tbsp. packed brown sugar, ½ tsp. crushed red pepper, 2 Tbsp. orange juice, and 1 tsp. orange zest. Stir until sugar dissolves. Stir in caramelized bananas.

garam masala chicken stew with peas and potatoes

PREP: 20 minutes | **PRESSURE COOK:** 17 minutes + time to build pressure | **STAND:** 15 minutes
MAKES: 6 servings (1 cup each)

Nonstick cooking spray

6 large skinless, boneless chicken thighs (about 1½ lb. total)

2 large red-skin potatoes, cut into ½-inch chunks (2 cups)

1 medium onion, thinly sliced

1½ tsp. grated fresh ginger

2 cloves garlic, minced

½ tsp. salt

½ tsp. black pepper

1 14.5-oz. can reduced-sodium chicken broth

1 8-oz. can no-salt-added tomato sauce

1 cup frozen peas

½ cup plain fat-free yogurt

1 to 1½ tsp. garam masala

1. Use a 4- to 6-qt. stove-top or electric pressure cooker. Lightly coat the inside of the pressure cooker with cooking spray. Heat over medium-high heat. (For an electric cooker, heat on sauté setting.) Add half the chicken to pressure cooker. Cook about 6 minutes or until browned on both sides; remove from pressure cooker. Repeat with remaining chicken. Drain off any fat.

2. Place potatoes, onion, ginger, and garlic in pressure cooker. Top with chicken. Sprinkle with salt and pepper. Pour broth and tomato sauce over mixture in cooker. Lock lid in place. Set electric cooker on high pressure to cook 12 minutes. For stove-top cooker, bring up to pressure over medium-high heat according to manufacturer's directions; reduce heat enough to maintain steady (but not excessive) pressure according to manufacturer's directions. Cook 12 minutes. Remove from heat. For electric and stove-top models, let stand to release pressure naturally at least 15 minutes or according to manufacturer's directions. If necessary, carefully open steam vent to release any remaining pressure. Open lid carefully.

3. Stir frozen peas, yogurt, and garam masala into chicken mixture in pressure cooker. Return stove-top cooker to medium heat and simmer, uncovered, 5 minutes. (Set electric cooker to simmer and cook, uncovered, 5 minutes.)

SLOW COOKER DIRECTIONS: Lightly coat a large skillet with cooking spray; heat skillet over medium-high heat. Add chicken; cook about 6 minutes or until browned on both sides. In a 3½- or 4-qt. slow cooker combine potatoes, onion, ginger, and garlic. Top with chicken. Sprinkle with salt and pepper. Pour broth and tomato sauce over mixture in cooker. Cover and cook on low 5½ hours or on high 2¾ hours. If using low, turn slow cooker to high. Stir in frozen peas, yogurt, and garam masala. Cover and cook 15 minutes more.

PER SERVING: *231 cal., 5 g fat (1 g sat. fat), 107 mg chol., 643 mg sodium, 19 g carb., 4 g fiber, 6 g sugars, 27 g pro.*

french chicken stew

PREP: 30 minutes | **PRESSURE COOK:** 8 minutes + time to build pressure | **STAND:** 15 minutes
MAKES: 8 servings (1 cup each)

4 cups sliced fresh button and/or stemmed shiitake mushrooms

1 14.5-oz. can diced tomatoes, undrained

1 cup thinly bias-sliced carrots

1 medium red-skin potato, cut into 1-inch pieces

½ cup chopped onion

½ cup fresh green beans, trimmed and cut into 1-inch pieces

½ cup pitted ripe olives, halved (tip, *right*)

1 cup reduced-sodium chicken broth

½ cup dry white wine or reduced-sodium chicken broth

1 tsp. dried herbes de Provence or Italian seasoning, crushed

¾ tsp. dried thyme, crushed

¼ tsp. coarsely ground black pepper

8 skinless, boneless chicken thighs (1¾ to 2 lb. total)

½ tsp. seasoned salt

1 14- to 16-oz. jar Alfredo pasta sauce

1. Combine all ingredients in a 6-qt. stove-top or electric pressure cooker. Lock lid in place. Set an electric cooker on high pressure to cook 8 minutes. For a stove-top cooker, bring up to pressure over medium-high heat according to manufacturer's directions; reduce heat enough to maintain steady (but not excessive) pressure according to manufacturer's directions. Cook 8 minutes. Remove from heat. For electric and stove-top models, let stand to release pressure naturally at least 15 minutes or according to manufacturer's directions. If necessary, carefully open steam vent to release any remaining pressure. Open lid carefully.

SLOW COOKER DIRECTIONS: In a 5- to 6-qt. slow cooker combine the first seven ingredients (through olives). Stir in broth, wine, herbes de Provence, thyme, and pepper. Top with chicken; sprinkle with seasoned salt. Cover and cook on low 6 to 7 hours or on high 3 to 4 hours. Stir in Alfredo sauce.

PER SERVING: *278 cal., 13 g fat (5 g sat. fat), 126 mg chol., 784 mg sodium, 13 g carb., 3 g fiber, 4 g sugars, 24 g pro.*

OLIVE UP

Want more olive flavor? Swap out the pitted ripe olives for Kalamata olives or Spanish green olives.

| FAST PREP

maple-plum duck breast

PREP: 20 minutes | **PRESSURE COOK:** 24 minutes + time to build pressure | **MAKES:** 4 servings

4 boneless duck breasts with skin (about 1¾ lb.) or 8 bone-in chicken thighs (about 3 lb.)

½ tsp. kosher salt

¼ tsp. freshly ground black pepper

1 Tbsp. vegetable oil

6 medium parsnips, peeled and cut into 2-inch chunks

4 shallots, halved or quartered (if large)

½ cup chicken broth

2 Tbsp. maple syrup

2 Tbsp. snipped fresh rosemary

2 cloves garlic, minced

4 fresh firm plums, halved

Fresh rosemary (optional)

1. Use a 6-qt. electric or stove-top pressure cooker. Score duck skin in a diamond pattern. Sprinkle duck with salt and pepper. For an electric pressure cooker, use the sauté setting to brown the duck, skin sides down, in hot oil (may omit oil if using duck). For a stove-top cooker, brown the duck, skin sides down, in hot oil directly in the cooker. Remove duck. Drain fat from cooker. Stir in the next six ingredients (through garlic). Place duck on top. Lock lid in place.

2. Set electric cooker on high pressure to cook 9 minutes for duck (or 10 minutes for chicken). For stove-top cooker, bring up to pressure over medium-high heat according to manufacturer's directions; reduce heat enough to maintain steady (but not excessive) pressure according to manufacturer's directions. Cook 9 minutes for duck or 10 minutes for chicken. Remove from heat. Quickly release pressure according to manufacturer's directions. Open lid carefully. Transfer duck and parsnip mixture to a serving dish; cover with foil to keep warm.

3. For the sauce, skim fat from the cooking liquid; discard fat. For electric cooker, turn on the sauté setting. For stove-top cooker, bring the liquid to boiling in the pressure cooker's pan; reduce the heat. For both electric and stove-top pressure cooker, boil gently, uncovered, about 15 minutes or until liquid is slightly syrupy, adding the plums during the last 5 minutes. Spoon the plum mixture over duck and parsnip mixture. Top with additional fresh rosemary.

SLOW COOKER DIRECTIONS: Prepare duck as directed. In a skillet heat oil over medium-high heat. Add duck, skin sides down; brown about 3 minutes. In a 4-qt. oval slow cooker combine the next six ingredients (through garlic). (If using chicken, use a 6-qt. slow cooker.) Place duck on top of vegetables. Cover and cook on low 5½ to 6½ hours or on high 2¾ to 3¼ hours or until an instant-read thermometer registers 165°F (175°F for chicken thighs). Transfer duck and parsnip mixture to a platter; cover to keep warm. Prepare sauce as directed, using a saucepan on the stove top. Serve as directed.

PER SERVING: *581 cal., 26 g fat (6 g sat. fat), 270 mg chol., 428 mg sodium, 36 g carb., 7 g fiber, 19 g sugars, 51 g pro.*

salmon with lentil hash and bacon

PREP: 20 minutes | **PRESSURE COOK:** 1 minute + time to build pressure
MAKES: 4 to 6 servings (5 oz. salmon + 1½ cups hash each)

1 1½-lb. fresh or frozen salmon fillet, skinned

2 cups reduced-sodium chicken broth

1 lb. baby yellow potatoes, quartered

1 small head cauliflower (1½ lb.), cut into large florets

1 cup dried brown lentils, rinsed and drained

1 large onion, cut into quarters

4 cloves garlic, minced

1 Tbsp. curry powder

½ tsp. kosher salt

½ tsp. ground cumin

½ tsp. ground coriander

¼ tsp. cayenne pepper

Kosher salt and black pepper

6 slices bacon, crisp-cooked, drained, and crumbled

Fresh mint leaves

1. Thaw fish, if frozen. Rinse fish; pat dry with paper towels. In a 6-qt. electric or stove-top pressure cooker stir together the next 11 ingredients (through cayenne pepper).

2. Cut the salmon fillet in half crosswise and place on top of the lentil mixture; sprinkle with salt and black pepper. Lock lid in place. Set electric cooker on high pressure to cook 1 minute to start the cooker. When cooker reaches that pressure, immediately release the pressure according to manufacturer's directions. For stove-top pressure cooker, bring up to pressure over medium-high heat according to manufacturer's directions. Remove from heat once it reaches that pressure. Quickly release the pressure according to manufacturer's directions. Open lid carefully.

3. Divide the salmon and vegetable mixture among four bowls. Top with crumbled bacon and fresh mint.

SLOW COOKER DIRECTIONS: In a 6-qt. slow cooker stir together broth and the next 10 ingredients (through cayenne pepper). Cover and cook on low 5 to 6 hours or on high 2½ to 3 hours. Meanwhile, thaw fish, if frozen. Rinse fish; pat dry with paper towels. Cut salmon fillet in half crosswise; sprinkle with salt and black pepper. Place salmon on top of vegetable mixture. If using low, turn cooker to high. Cover and cook about 25 minutes more or just until fish flakes. Serve as directed.

PER SERVING: 623 cal., 16 g fat (3 g sat. fat), 105 mg chol., 768 mg sodium, 63 g carb., 13 g fiber, 8 g sugars, 57 g pro.

spring german potato salad

PREP: 30 minutes | **PRESSURE COOK:** 5 minutes + time to build pressure | **STAND:** 15 minutes
MAKES: 12 side-dish servings (½ cup potato mixture + ½ cup greens each)

 6 slices thick bacon, chopped
 2 lb. tiny red-skin and/or yellow new potatoes, halved
 1 cup sliced green onions, ramps, or leeks
 ½ cup sliced celery
 ⅓ cup cider vinegar
 ⅓ cup water
 2 Tbsp. sugar
 2 tsp. spicy brown mustard
 1 tsp. salt
 ¼ tsp. celery seeds
 ¼ tsp. black pepper
 6 cups mixed baby greens or baby spinach
 1 Tbsp. snipped fresh dill weed

1. Use a 4- to 6-qt. stove-top or electric pressure cooker. For an electric pressure cooker, heat on sauté setting; for a stove-top cooker, heat over medium-high heat. Add bacon to pressure cooker and cook until crisp. Drain bacon on paper towels. Reserve 1 Tbsp. bacon drippings in cooker; discard remaining drippings.

2. Add potatoes, green onions, and celery to the reserved drippings in cooker. Combine the next seven ingredients (through pepper). Pour over potato mixture. Lock lid in place. Set electric pressure cooker on high pressure to cook 5 minutes. For stove-top cookers, bring up to pressure over medium-high heat according to manufacturer's directions; reduce heat enough to maintain steady (but not excessive) pressure according to manufacturer's directions. Cook 5 minutes. Remove from heat. For electric and stove-top models, let stand to release pressure naturally at least 15 minutes or according to manufacturer's directions. If necessary, carefully open steam vent to release any remaining pressure. Open lid carefully.

3. Serve warm potato salad over baby greens. Sprinkle with reserved bacon and dill weed.

SLOW COOKER DIRECTIONS: In a medium skillet cook bacon over medium heat until crisp. Drain bacon on paper towels. Set aside 1 Tbsp. bacon drippings; discard remaining drippings. In a 3½- or 4-qt. cooker combine potatoes, green onions, and celery. In a small bowl combine the reserved bacon drippings and the next seven ingredients (through pepper). Pour over potato mixture in cooker. Cover and cook on low 8 hours or on high 4 hours or until tender. Serve as directed.

PER SERVING: 110 cal., 4 g fat (1 g sat. fat), 6 mg chol., 340 mg sodium, 16 g carb., 2 g fiber, 3 g sugars, 4 g pro.

**Tomato-Basil Cavatelli
Skillet,** *page 256*

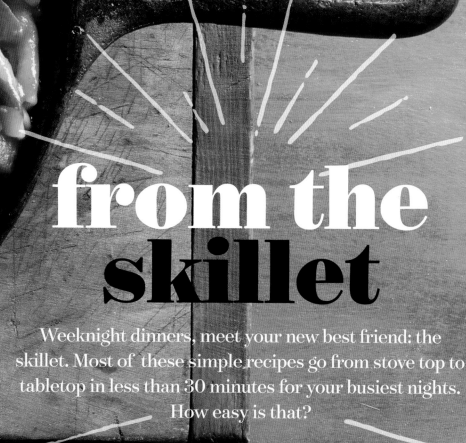

from the skillet

Weeknight dinners, meet your new best friend: the skillet. Most of these simple recipes go from stove top to tabletop in less than 30 minutes for your busiest nights. How easy is that?

greek flat iron steaks

START TO FINISH: 25 minutes | **MAKES:** 4 servings (3 oz. steak + ½ cup tomatoes each)

1 lemon

2 6- to 8-oz. boneless beef shoulder top blade (flat iron) steaks, trimmed of fat (tip, *right*)

Salt and black pepper

1 tsp. dried rosemary, crushed

4 tsp. olive oil

2 cups grape tomatoes, halved if desired

2 cloves garlic, minced

⅓ cup pitted green olives, halved

¼ cup crumbled feta cheese (1 oz.)

1. Finely shred 1 tsp. zest from the lemon. Cut lemon into wedges. Set zest and wedges aside. Cut each steak in half and generously season both sides with salt and pepper. Sprinkle rosemary evenly over both sides of steaks; rub in with your fingers.

2. In a large nonstick skillet heat 2 tsp. of the oil over medium-high heat. Add steaks; cook 8 to 10 minutes or until medium rare (145°F), turning once. Remove steaks from skillet; cover to keep warm.

3. Add the remaining 2 tsp. oil to skillet. Add tomatoes and garlic; cook over medium-high heat about 3 minutes or until tomatoes start to soften and burst. Remove from heat. Stir in olives and the reserved lemon zest.

4. Serve steaks with tomato mixture and the reserved lemon wedges. Sprinkle with cheese.

PER SERVING: 220 cal., 13 g fat (4 g sat. fat), 56 mg chol., 467 mg sodium, 6 g carb., 2 g fiber, 3 g sugars, 20 g pro.

STEAK IT OUT

Prized for being lean, tender, and inexpensive, flat iron steaks come from the chuck (shoulder) section of beef. If you can't find this cut, you can substitute eye round, tri-tip, or top loin (strip) steak.

FAST PREP

lemon-thyme roasted chicken with fingerlings

START TO FINISH: 30 minutes | **MAKES:** 4 servings (1 breast half + ¾ cup potatoes each)

4 tsp. canola oil or olive oil

1 tsp. dried thyme, crushed

½ tsp. kosher salt or ¼ tsp. regular salt

¼ tsp. freshly ground black pepper

1 lb. fingerling potatoes, halved lengthwise, and/ or tiny new red or white potatoes, halved

4 skinless, boneless chicken breast halves (1 to 1¼ lb. total)

2 cloves garlic, minced

1 lemon, thinly sliced

Fresh thyme (optional)

1. In an extra-large skillet heat 2 tsp. of the oil over medium heat. Stir in ½ tsp. of the dried thyme, the salt, and pepper. Add potatoes; toss gently to coat. Cover and cook 12 minutes, stirring twice.

2. Stir potatoes; push to one side of skillet. Add the remaining 2 tsp. oil to the other side of skillet. Arrange chicken in skillet alongside the potatoes. Cook, uncovered, 5 minutes.

3. Turn chicken. Sprinkle with garlic and the remaining ½ tsp. dried thyme; top with lemon slices. Cover and cook 7 to 10 minutes more or until chicken is no longer pink (165°F) and potatoes are tender. If desired, top with fresh thyme.

PER SERVING: *255 cal., 6 g fat (1 g sat. fat), 66 mg chol., 307 mg sodium, 21 g carb., 3 g fiber, 1 g sugars, 29 g pro.*

THE WORD "CACCIATORE" REFERS TO ANY DISH MADE "HUNTER-STYLE," WHICH USUALLY INCLUDES MUSHROOMS, HERBS, TOMATOES, AND WINE.

chicken cacciatore

PREP: 30 minutes | **COOK:** 15 minutes | **MAKES:** 4 servings (2 thighs + 1¼ cups vegetables each)

8 small bone-in chicken thighs (about 2 lb. total), skin removed

Salt and coarsely ground black pepper

1 Tbsp. olive oil

3 cups sliced fresh cremini mushrooms (8 oz.)

1 large yellow or green sweet pepper, cut into bite-size strips

⅓ cup finely chopped carrot

3 cloves garlic, minced

½ cup dry white wine or chicken broth

1 28-oz. can diced tomatoes, undrained

1½ cups frozen small whole onions

1 tsp. coarsely ground black pepper

1 tsp. dried oregano, crushed

2 Tbsp. balsamic vinegar

10 pitted Kalamata olives, chopped if desired (optional)

⅓ cup snipped fresh Italian parsley (optional)

1. Sprinkle chicken lightly with salt and black pepper. In a large skillet heat oil over medium heat. Add chicken; cook just until browned on both sides. Remove chicken from skillet.

2. Add mushrooms, sweet pepper, carrot, and garlic to skillet; cook and stir 4 minutes. Carefully add wine. Simmer, uncovered, until liquid is nearly evaporated. Stir in the next four ingredients (through oregano).

3. Return chicken to skillet. Bring to boiling; reduce heat. Simmer, covered, 15 minutes or until chicken is done (at least 175°F). Stir in vinegar. Season to taste with additional salt. If desired, sprinkle with olives and parsley before serving.

TO MAKE AHEAD: Prepare as directed. Place chicken and sauce in a large bowl or storage container. Cover and refrigerate up to 3 days. Return chicken and sauce to the skillet. Cover and cook over medium heat until heated through, stirring occasionally.

PER SERVING: *317 cal., 9 g fat (2 g sat. fat), 129 mg chol., 609 mg sodium, 23 g carb., 4 g fiber, 11 g sugars, 31 g pro.*

| FAST PREP

mediterranean pizza skillet

START TO FINISH: 30 minutes | **MAKES:** 4 servings (2½ cups each)

- 2 Tbsp. olive oil
- 1 lb. skinless, boneless chicken breast halves, cut into ¾-inch pieces
- 2 cloves garlic, minced
- 1 14-oz. can quartered artichoke hearts, drained
- 1⅓ cups chopped roma tomatoes (4 medium)
- 1 2.25-oz. can sliced pitted ripe olives, drained
- ½ tsp. dried Italian seasoning, crushed
- ¼ tsp. black pepper
- 2 cups romaine lettuce or mesclun mix, chopped
- 1 cup crumbled feta cheese (4 oz.)
- ⅓ cup fresh basil leaves, shredded or torn

  Crusty Italian or French bread slices, toasted

1. In a large skillet heat oil over medium-high heat. Add chicken and garlic; cook and stir 2 to 4 minutes or until chicken is browned. Stir in the next five ingredients (through pepper). Bring to boiling; reduce heat. Simmer, covered, about 10 minutes or until chicken is no longer pink.

2. Top chicken mixture with lettuce and cheese. Cook, covered, 1 to 2 minutes more or just until lettuce begins to wilt. Sprinkle with basil. Serve on or with toasted bread slices.

PER SERVING: 395 cal., 17 g fat (6 g sat. fat), 82 mg chol., 1,003 mg sodium, 27 g carb., 6 g fiber, 5 g sugars, 33 g pro.

weeknight paella

START TO FINISH: 20 minutes | **MAKES:** 4 servings (1¼ cups each)

8 oz. fresh or frozen sea scallops

8 oz. fresh or frozen peeled and deveined cooked shrimp

1 10-oz. pkg. frozen long grain white rice with vegetables (peas, corn, and carrots)

½ to 1 tsp. ground turmeric

1 Tbsp. canola oil

1⅓ cups coarsely chopped roma tomatoes (4 medium)

Salt and black pepper

Snipped fresh Italian parsley (optional)

1. Thaw scallops and shrimp, if frozen. Rinse scallops and shrimp; pat dry with paper towels. Cut any large scallops in half. Prepare rice according to package directions. Stir in turmeric.

2. Meanwhile, in a large skillet heat oil over medium heat. Add scallops; cook about 3 minutes or until scallops are opaque, turning once. Stir in shrimp and tomatoes; heat through.

3. Add hot rice to seafood mixture in skillet; toss gently to combine. Season to taste with salt and pepper. If desired, sprinkle with parsley.

PER SERVING: *229 cal., 5 g fat (1 g sat. fat), 129 mg chol., 374 mg sodium, 22 g carb., 2 g fiber, 3 g sugars, 24 g pro.*

ALL ABOUT SCALLOPS

What we call a scallop is really the adductor muscle of the bivalve mollusk of the same name. Look for scallops that are creamy beige to light pink in color.

fish veracruz

START TO FINISH: 25 minutes | **MAKES:** 4 servings (1 piece fish + 1 cup sauce each)

4   6- to 8-oz. fresh or frozen skinless tilapia, mahi mahi, or other fish fillets

1   Tbsp. olive oil

1   small onion, cut into thin wedges

1   jalapeño chile pepper, seeded and finely chopped (tip, *page 14*) (optional)

1   clove garlic, minced

1   14.5-oz. can diced tomatoes, undrained

1   cup sliced fresh cremini or button mushrooms

¾   cup pimiento-stuffed olives, coarsely chopped

1   Tbsp. snipped fresh oregano or ½ tsp. dried oregano, crushed

¼   tsp. salt

⅛   tsp. black pepper

2   cups hot cooked rice and/or 8 crusty bread slices (optional)

1. Thaw fish, if frozen. Rinse fish; pat dry with paper towels. Set fish aside.

2. For sauce, in an extra-large skillet heat oil over medium heat. Add onion, chile pepper (if using), and garlic; cook and stir 2 to 3 minutes or until onion is tender. Add the next six ingredients (through black pepper) to the skillet. Bring to boiling.

3. Gently place fish in sauce in skillet, spooning sauce over fish. Return to boiling; reduce heat. Simmer, covered, 8 to 10 minutes or until fish flakes easily. Using a wide spatula, carefully lift fish from skillet to a serving dish. Spoon sauce over fish. If desired, serve with rice.

PER SERVING: *267 cal., 11 g fat (2 g sat. fat), 85 mg chol., 928 mg sodium, 9 g carb., 3 g fiber, 4 g sugars, 36 g pro.*

WHY TILAPIA?

Tilapia has been a staple in Africa for ages and is now mainstream in the United States because it's low in fat, versatile, readily available, and inexpensive, thanks to much of its production coming from farming methods.

FAST PREP

tomato-basil cavatelli skillet

PREP: 15 minutes | **COOK:** 20 minutes | **STAND:** 10 minutes | **MAKES:** 4 servings (1⅔ cups each)

1 28-oz. can whole peeled tomatoes, undrained and cut up

12 oz. dried cavatelli, gemelli, or rotini pasta

1 14.5-oz. can reduced-sodium chicken broth or vegetable broth

¼ cup water

3 cloves garlic, minced

1 tsp. dried Italian seasoning, crushed

½ cup fresh basil leaves, coarsely chopped or torn

2 Tbsp. olive oil

½ tsp. kosher salt

¼ to ½ tsp. crushed red pepper

8 oz. sliced fresh mozzarella or shredded mozzarella cheese (2 cups)

1. In a deep large skillet layer undrained tomatoes and the next nine ingredients (through crushed red pepper) in the order listed. Do not stir. Bring to boiling over medium-high heat; reduce heat. Simmer, covered, 20 minutes or until pasta is tender, stirring occasionally.

2. Remove lid and top with cheese. Cover and let stand 10 minutes before serving. If desired, sprinkle with additional fresh basil.

PER SERVING: 568 cal., 18 g fat (7 g sat. fat), 40 mg chol., 999 mg sodium, 73 g carb., 6 g fiber, 7 g sugars, 24 g pro.

Spicy Cheesy Succotash, *page 266*

on the side

Easy side dishes are key when time is short,
but the real trick is keeping them exciting.
These recipes will get you there—quick!

| FAST PREP

2 ways with quinoa

START TO FINISH: 20 minutes | **MAKES:** 4 servings

1½ cups reduced-sodium
chicken broth or vegetable
broth or water

2 cloves garlic, minced

¾ cup quinoa (white, red, or
multicolor)

1. In a medium saucepan bring broth and garlic to boiling. Meanwhile, rinse and drain quinoa. Slowly stir quinoa into the broth and return to boiling; reduce heat. Simmer, covered, about 15 minutes or until quinoa reaches desired tenderness. Drain if necessary.

GREEK QUINOA *(BELOW LEFT):* After cooking quinoa, add halved or chopped cherry tomatoes, chopped pitted Kalamata olives, crumbled feta cheese, and snipped fresh baby spinach. Sprinkle with Greek seasoning. Drizzle with olive oil and freshly squeezed lemon juice to taste. Toss gently with a fork.

ITALIAN QUINOA *(BELOW RIGHT):* After cooking quinoa, add halved or chopped cherry tomatoes, fresh mozzarella pearls (or cubed fresh mozzarella), and black pepper to taste. Drizzle with bottled Italian salad dressing. Toss gently with a fork.

2 ways with bulgur

START TO FINISH: 20 minutes | **MAKES:** 4 servings

2 cups reduced-sodium chicken broth or vegetable broth or water

1 cup bulgur

1. In a medium saucepan combine broth and bulgur. Bring to boiling; reduce heat. Simmer, covered, about 15 minutes or until tender. Drain if necessary.

SPICED BULGUR PILAF *(BELOW LEFT)*: After cooking bulgur, add golden raisins, toasted sliced almonds, and sliced green onions. Drizzle with olive oil and freshly squeezed lemon juice to moisten. Add ground cinnamon and snipped fresh mint to taste. Toss gently with a fork.

WARM CINNAMON-APPLE BULGUR *(BELOW RIGHT)*: Cook bulgur in water. After cooking, add golden raisins, chopped apple, and toasted sliced almonds. Drizzle with maple syrup to moisten. Add ground cinnamon to taste. Toss gently with a fork.

2 ways with farro

START TO FINISH: 30 minutes | **MAKES:** 4 servings

3 cups reduced-sodium chicken broth or vegetable broth

1 cup pearled farro

1. In a medium saucepan combine broth and farro. Bring to boiling; reduce heat. Simmer, covered, 25 to 30 minutes or until tender. Drain if necessary.

ORANGE-SPINACH FARRO (*BELOW LEFT*): After cooking farro, add torn fresh baby spinach, cut-up orange sections, chopped dried cranberries, and chopped toasted walnuts. Drizzle with olive oil. Add snipped fresh rosemary and black pepper to taste. Toss gently with a fork.

ORANGE-CHERRY FARRO SALAD (*BELOW RIGHT*): After cooking farro, add cut-up orange sections, chopped dried cherries, and chopped apple. Drizzle with bottled poppy seed salad dressing to taste. Toss gently with a fork.

2 ways with barley

START TO FINISH: 15 minutes | **MAKES:** 4 servings

3   cups reduced-sodium chicken broth or vegetable broth

1¼ cups quick-cooking pearled barley

1. In a medium saucepan bring broth to boiling. Slowly stir in barley. Return to boiling; reduce heat. Simmer, covered, about 10 minutes or until tender. Drain if necessary.

MANGO-CHIPOTLE BARLEY *(BELOW LEFT)***:** After cooking barley, add chopped, peeled mango; thawed frozen corn; rinsed and drained black beans; snipped fresh cilantro; and minced canned chipotle chile pepper. Drizzle with freshly squeezed lime juice to taste. If desired, add 1 tsp. adobo sauce from the chipotle chile peppers. Toss gently with a fork.

ONE-POT TACO BARLEY *(BELOW RIGHT)***:** After cooking barley, add thawed frozen corn, shredded cooked chicken or crumbled cooked ground beef, cheddar cheese cubes, and torn romaine lettuce. Add taco seasoning to taste. Toss gently with a fork. Top with crushed tortilla chips.

baked beans with bacon

PREP: 30 minutes | **STAND:** 1 hour | **COOK:** 1 hour | **BAKE:** 1 hour 30 minutes at 300°F
MAKES: 10 to 12 servings (½ cup each)

- 1 lb. dried navy beans or Great Northern beans (2⅓ cups)
- 4 oz. bacon or pancetta, chopped
- 1 cup chopped onion
- ¼ cup packed brown sugar
- ⅓ cup molasses or pure maple syrup
- ¼ cup Worcestershire sauce
- 1½ tsp. dry mustard
- ½ tsp. salt
- ¼ tsp. black pepper

1. Rinse beans. In an oven-safe 4- to 5-qt. pot combine beans and 8 cups water. Bring to boiling; reduce heat. Simmer, uncovered, 2 minutes. Remove from heat. Cover; let stand 1 hour. Drain and rinse.

2. Return beans to pot. Add 8 cups fresh water. Bring to boiling; reduce heat. Simmer, covered, 60 to 90 minutes or until beans are tender, stirring occasionally. Drain beans, reserving liquid.

3. Preheat oven to 300°F. In the same pot cook bacon and onion over medium heat until bacon is slightly crisp and onion is tender, stirring occasionally. Add brown sugar; cook and stir until sugar is dissolved. Stir in molasses, Worcestershire sauce, dry mustard, salt, and pepper. Stir in drained beans and 1¼ cups of the reserved bean liquid.

4. Bake, covered, 60 minutes. Uncover and bake 30 to 45 minutes more or until desired consistency, stirring occasionally. Beans will thicken slightly as they cool. If necessary, stir in additional reserved bean liquid. If desired, sprinkle with additional cooked chopped bacon or pancetta.

PER SERVING: *267 cal., 6 g fat (2 g sat. fat), 8 mg chol., 282 mg sodium, 43 g carb., 11 g fiber, 0 g sugars, 12 g pro.*

BAKED BEANS WITH BACON, STEP-BY-STEP

1. Beans can be dirty. Sort through the package of beans and remove any pebbles and broken or shriveled beans. Rinse thoroughly in a colander.
2. Soaking dried beans helps the beans soften slightly, allowing them to cook quicker. Water starts to seep into the bean where it was attached to the plant. Soak beans overnight or use the universal quick-soak method in the recipe.
3. Beans will plump slightly after soaking. After you drain the beans, toss the soaking liquid and use fresh water for cooking.
4. Baking the beans with the lid off allows the excess liquid to evaporate and the sauce to thicken. When the beans are as saucy or as thick as you like, they're ready to serve!

indian-scented roasted beets and carrots

PREP: 25 minutes | **SLOW COOK:** 4 to 5 hours (high)
MAKES: 10 servings (¾ cup vegetables + 1 Tbsp. cream each)

2½ lb. medium beets, trimmed, peeled, and cut into wedges (6 cups)

8 oz. medium carrots, halved crosswise

¼ cup olive oil

¾ tsp. kosher salt

¼ tsp. black pepper

1 lime

1 Tbsp. honey

1 clove garlic, minced

½ tsp. ground coriander

½ tsp. ground cumin

¼ tsp. crushed red pepper

1 6-oz. carton plain Greek yogurt

¼ cup snipped fresh cilantro

1 tsp. grated fresh ginger

1. Place beets in the center of a piece of heavy foil. Place carrots on another piece of foil. Drizzle vegetables with 2 Tbsp. of the oil and sprinkle with ¼ tsp. of the salt and the black pepper. Wrap tightly in foil and stack in a 6-qt. slow cooker. Cover and cook on high 4 to 5 hours or until tender.

2. Meanwhile, remove ½ tsp. zest and squeeze 1 Tbsp. juice from the lime. Set zest aside. For dressing, in a small bowl whisk together the lime juice, the remaining 2 Tbsp. oil, remaining ½ tsp. salt, the honey, garlic, coriander, cumin, and crushed red pepper.

3. Remove foil packets from cooker. Open packets, reserving liquid. Cut carrots into thin strips. Place beets, carrots, and liquid from packets in the cooker. Drizzle with the dressing; toss to coat.

4. For lime-cilantro cream, in a small bowl combine lime zest, yogurt, cilantro, and ginger. Serve vegetables with the cream and, if desired, sprinkle with additional crushed red pepper.

PER SERVING: 127 cal., 6 g fat (1 g sat. fat), 1 mg chol., 258 mg sodium, 16 g carb., 4 g fiber, 11 g sugars, 4 g pro.

mashed sweet potatoes with mushooms and bacon

PREP: 40 minutes | **COOK:** 20 minutes | **MAKES:** 10 servings (¾ cup each)

- 6 slices bacon, chopped
- 8 oz. cremini mushrooms, halved (quartered if large)
- 1 medium red onion, cut into thin wedges
- 2 Tbsp. lemon juice
- ⅓ cup golden raisins
- 3 lb. orange-flesh sweet potatoes, peeled and cut up
- ½ cup milk
- 2 Tbsp. butter
- 1 tsp. kosher salt

1. In a 6-qt. pot cook bacon over medium heat 8 to 10 minutes or until crisp. Drain bacon on paper towels, reserving 3 Tbsp. drippings in pot. Add mushrooms and onion to drippings. Cook and stir over medium heat 8 minutes or until mushrooms are tender and browned. Drizzle with lemon juice. Stir the cooked bacon and the raisins into the mushroom mixture. Transfer to a bowl; cover with foil to keep warm.

2. Wipe out the pot. Add sweet potatoes and enough salted water to cover. Bring to boiling. Cook potatoes, covered, 20 to 25 minutes or until tender. Drain; return to pot. Using a potato masher or fork, mash potatoes. Stir in milk, butter, and salt until butter melts. Stir in mushroom mixture or stir in half of the mushroom mixture and top with remaining half.

TO MAKE AHEAD: Prepare as directed, stirring all of the mushroom mixture into mashed sweet potatoes. Transfer mixture to a storage container; cover and chill up to 24 hours. To serve, return sweet potatoes to the pot; heat through.

PER SERVING: *226 cal., 8 g fat (4 g sat. fat), 15 mg chol., 379 mg sodium, 34 g carb., 5 g fiber, 10 g sugars, 5 g pro.*

no-knead bread

PREP: 25 minutes | STAND: 4 hours | RISE: 1 hour | BAKE: 40 minutes at 450°F | MAKES: 10 servings (1 slice each)

3 cups all-purpose flour

1¼ tsp. salt

¼ tsp. active dry yeast

1⅔ cups warm water (120°F to 130°F)

5 Tbsp. all-purpose flour

1 Tbsp. yellow cornmeal

1. In a large bowl combine the 3 cups flour, the salt, and yeast. Add the warm water. Stir until flour mixture is moistened (dough will be very sticky and soft). Cover; let stand at room temperature 4 to 24 hours.

2. Generously sprinkle additional flour (3 to 4 Tbsp.) on a large piece of parchment paper. Turn dough out onto floured paper. Sprinkle top of dough mixture lightly with additional flour (1 to 2 Tbsp.); using a large spatula, gently fold dough over onto itself. Sprinkle lightly with additional flour (1 to 2 Tbsp.). Cover; let rest 15 minutes.

3. Grease an oven-safe 5- to 6-qt. heavy pot with a diameter of 8½ to 9½ inches; sprinkle cornmeal over bottom and about 2 inches up the sides. Gently turn dough into prepared pot, using a spatula to help scrape dough off the paper (some dough may remain on the paper). Cover; let rise at room temperature until dough has risen by about 1 inch (1 to 2 hours).

4. Preheat oven to 450°F. Cover pot with a lid or foil; bake 30 minutes. Uncover; bake 10 to 15 minutes more or until top is golden brown. Immediately remove bread from pot. Cool completely on a wire rack.

PER SERVING: *154 cal., 0 g fat, 0 mg chol., 293 mg sodium, 32 g carb., 1 g fiber, 0 g sugars, 4 g pro.*

NO-KNEAD BREAD, STEP-BY-STEP

1. The dough for this bread is very soft, so it doesn't get kneaded, but it does need a little more flour worked in. Use a stiff spatula to scrape dough onto floured parchment.

2. Sprinkle the top of the dough with flour. Use the spatula to lift and fold the dough over. You don't want to overwork the dough (as with kneading).

3. Slide a baking sheet under the parchment to support it. Hold the paper in place with your thumb and scrape dough off paper into the prepared pot.

| FAST PREP

bacon corn bread

PREP: 15 minutes | **BAKE:** 20 minutes at 350°F | **MAKES:** 8 to 10 servings (1 wedge each)

⅓   cup butter

¾   cup milk

2   eggs, lightly beaten

½   cup frozen whole kernel corn

1   cup yellow cornmeal

¾   cup all-purpose flour

⅓   cup sugar

1   Tbsp. baking powder

¾   tsp. salt

1   2.8- to 3-oz. pkg. cooked
    bacon pieces

¾   to 1 cup shredded cheddar
    cheese (3 to 4 oz.)

1. Preheat oven to 350°F. In an oven-safe 3½- or 4-qt. nonstick pot with a 7½- to 8½-inch diameter, melt butter over medium heat. Immediately remove pot from heat.

2. Add milk, eggs, and corn to butter in pot; stir to combine. Add the next five ingredients (through salt). Stir just until moistened (batter should be lumpy [tip, *below*]). Stir in half of the bacon pieces (⅓ cup) and ½ cup of the cheese. Sprinkle remaining bacon and cheese over top.

3. Bake 20 to 25 minutes or until a toothpick comes out clean. Serve warm.

PER SERVING: *327 cal., 16 g fat (8 g sat. fat), 87 mg chol., 865 mg sodium, 35 g carb., 1 g fiber, 10 g sugars, 12 g pro.*

STIR WITH CARE

The secret to moist, tender corn bread? Avoid overmixing. Stir the wet and dry ingredients together just until combined. The batter should be a little lumpy when the corn bread goes into the oven.

pesto monkey bread

PREP: 15 minutes | **SLOW COOK:** 2 hours 10 minutes (high) | **COOL:** 30 minutes | **MAKES:** 10 servings (2 rolls each)

Foil-lined parchment pan-lining paper

¼ cup grated Parmesan cheese

½ tsp. dried Italian seasoning, crushed

2 Tbsp. butter, melted

2 Tbsp. purchased pesto

2 7.5-oz. cans refrigerated buttermilk biscuits (20 biscuits)

Marinara sauce (optional)

1. Line a 3½- or 4-qt. oval slow cooker with a double thickness of pan-lining paper, parchment sides facing the food. In a small bowl combine Parmesan cheese and Italian seasoning. In another small bowl whisk together butter and pesto.

2. Pull and pinch each dough piece into a ball. Arrange 10 balls in paper-lined slow cooker, starting in the center and working toward the edge, leaving a little space between pieces. Sprinkle with half of the cheese mixture and half of the butter mixture. Repeat layers.

3. Cover and cook on high 1½ hours; rotate the removable crockery liner. Cover and cook 40 to 50 minutes more or until an instant-read thermometer inserted in the center registers 200°F. Using the edges of the paper, transfer bread to a wire rack; cool slightly. Serve bread warm and, if desired, with marinara sauce.

PER SERVING: *143 cal., 6 g fat (2 g sat. fat), 9 mg chol., 460 mg sodium, 20 g carb., 1 g fiber, 3 g sugars, 4 g pro.*

Pear Cheese Tumble, *page 286*

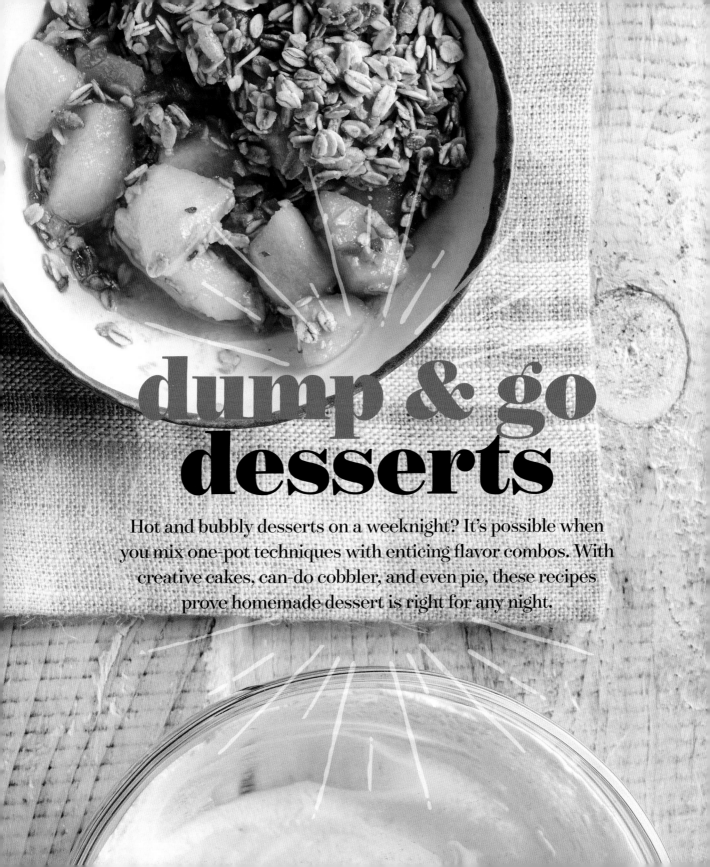

dump & go
desserts

Hot and bubbly desserts on a weeknight? It's possible when you mix one-pot techniques with enticing flavor combos. With creative cakes, can-do cobbler, and even pie, these recipes prove homemade dessert is right for any night.

FAST PREP

mixed-berry cobbler

PREP: 15 minutes | **BAKE:** 20 minutes at 400°F | **MAKES:** 6 servings

1 21-oz. can cherry pie filling

1½ cups fresh or frozen blackberries

1½ cups fresh or frozen raspberries

1 cup fresh or frozen blueberries

½ cup flaked coconut

2 tsp. lime zest

1 7.5-oz. pkg. refrigerated biscuits (10 biscuits)

Milk or melted butter

2 Tbsp. flaked coconut

1. Preheat oven to 400°F. In an oven-safe 3- to 4-qt. pot or saucepan stir together pie filling, blackberries, raspberries, blueberries, the ½ cup coconut, and 1 tsp. of the lime zest. Bring to boiling over medium heat. Remove pot from heat.

2. Separate biscuits and arrange on top of hot fruit mixture. Brush with milk and sprinkle with the 2 Tbsp. coconut and the remaining 1 tsp. lime zest.

3. Bake, uncovered, 25 to 30 minutes or until biscuits are golden. Cool slightly before serving.

PER SERVING: *305 cal., 6 g fat (3 g sat. fat), 1 mg chol., 388 mg sodium, 59 g carb., 6 g fiber, 11 g sugars, 4 g pro.*

peach-berry slump

PREP: 15 minutes | **BAKE:** 1 hour 15 minutes at 350°F | **MAKES:** 8 servings

1 cup all-purpose flour

⅔ cup sugar

1½ tsp. baking powder

½ tsp. ground cinnamon

¼ tsp. salt

½ cup milk

2 Tbsp. butter, melted

1 tsp. vanilla

½ cup water

½ cup sugar

1 16-oz. pkg. frozen sliced peaches

2 cups frozen raspberries

Dulce de leche ice cream (optional)

1. Preheat oven to 350°F. In a medium bowl stir together the first five ingredients (through salt). Add milk, butter, and vanilla; stir just until combined. Set batter aside.

2. In an oven-safe 4- to 5-qt. pot combine the water and the ½ cup sugar. Cook and stir over medium-high heat until sugar dissolves. Pour into a glass measuring cup. Add peaches and berries to the pot; Spread batter evenly over fruit (it may not completely cover fruit). Drizzle sugar-water over batter.

3. Bake, uncovered, 75 minutes or until a toothpick comes out clean. Cool slightly. Serve warm. If desired, top with ice cream.

PER SERVING: 245 cal., 4 g fat (2 g sat. fat), 9 mg chol., 196 mg sodium, 52 g carb., 3 g fiber, 36 g sugars, 3 g pro.

smoky apple-cherry pot pie

PREP: 30 minutes | **BAKE:** 1 hour 20 minutes at 375°F | **COOL:** 30 minutes | **MAKES:** 8 servings

8 cups thinly sliced peeled apples

4 cups frozen pitted tart red cherries

1 cup sugar

¼ cup all-purpose flour

½ tsp. smoked paprika (optional)

½ of a 14.1-oz. pkg. rolled refrigerated unbaked piecrust (1 crust)

Milk (optional)

Coarse sugar (optional)

1. Preheat oven to 375°F. Place apples and cherries in an oven-safe 5- to 6-qt. pot with a diameter of about 10 inches. Add the 1 cup sugar, the flour, and, if desired, paprika; stir to coat. Place crust on top of filling; cut slits in crust for steam to escape. If desired, brush crust with milk and sprinkle with coarse sugar.

2. Bake, uncovered, 80 minutes or until filling is bubbly in center and crust is golden (if crust browns too quickly, tent with foil). Cool at least 30 minutes before serving. Serve warm or cool completely.

PER SERVING: *305 cal., 7 g fat (3 g sat. fat), 2 mg chol., 132 mg sodium, 64 g carb., 4 g fiber, 43 g sugars, 2 g pro.*

THIS FRUIT-FILLED POT PIE IS A FUN RIFF ON THE SAVORY CLASSIC. THE ADDITION OF SMOKED PAPRIKA GIVES IT A SAVORY, EARTHY UNDERTONE, BUT IF YOU PREFER, YOU CAN USE CINNAMON OR APPLE PIE SPICE IN ITS PLACE.

banana–chocolate chip wacky cake

PREP: 20 minutes | **BAKE:** 30 minutes at 350°F | **MAKES:** 8 servings

1½ cups all-purpose flour

¾ cup packed brown sugar

1 tsp. baking soda

¼ tsp. salt

6 Tbsp. butter

⅔ cup mashed ripe bananas (2 medium)

¼ cup milk

1 Tbsp. vinegar

½ cup miniature semisweet chocolate pieces

⅓ cup chopped mixed nuts or pecans (optional)

Ice cream (optional)

Chocolate-flavor ice cream topping (optional)

1. Preheat oven to 350°F. Combine the first four ingredients (through salt). In a shallow oven-safe 4- to 5-qt. pot melt butter over medium-low heat. Remove pot from heat. Stir in bananas, milk, and vinegar just until combined, stirring to edges of pan. Stir in the flour mixture. Sprinkle with chocolate pieces and, if desired, nuts.

2. Bake, uncovered, 30 to 35 minutes or until a toothpick comes out clean (center may dip slightly). Cool in pot on a wire rack. If desired, serve with ice cream and chocolate topping.

PER SERVING: *351 cal., 13 g fat (8 g sat. fat), 24 mg chol., 309 mg sodium, 55 g carb., 1 g fiber, 32 g sugars, 4 g pro.*

IS IT DONE?

Once the minimum baking time is reached, use a toothpick to check the cake for doneness. The toothpick should come out clean or with just a few crumbs stuck to it. If there is any wet batter on it, bake the cake a few minutes longer and test again in a new spot with a clean toothpick.

| FAST PREP

lemon-poppy seed cake

PREP: 10 minutes | **BAKE:** 20 minutes at 350°F | **COOL:** 1 hour | **MAKES:** 12 servings

- 3 Tbsp. butter
- 1 cup buttermilk
- 1 egg, lightly beaten
- 1 tsp. vanilla
- 1½ cups all-purpose flour
- ½ cup sugar
- ¼ cup cornmeal
- 1 Tbsp. poppy seeds
- 1 tsp. baking soda
- 1 tsp. lemon zest (tip, *right*)
- ½ tsp. salt
  Powdered Sugar Icing
  (optional)

1. Preheat oven to 350°F. In an oven-safe 4- to 5-qt. pot with a 7½- to 8-inch diameter melt butter over medium-low heat. Stir in buttermilk, egg, and vanilla until combined. Stir in the remaining ingredients except icing until smooth.

2. Bake, uncovered, 20 to 30 minutes or until a toothpick comes out clean. Serve warm or cool completely. If desired, drizzle with Powdered Sugar Icing.

PER SERVING: 145 cal., 4 g fat (2 g sat. fat), 24 mg chol., 252 mg sodium, 24 g carb., 1 g fiber, 10 g sugars, 3 g pro.

POWDERED SUGAR ICING: In a small bowl combine 1½ cups powdered sugar, ¼ tsp. vanilla or almond extract, and 2 Tbsp. milk. If necessary, add additional milk (up to 2 Tbsp.) to make icing drizzling consistency.

CITRUS SWITCH

Lemon and poppy seeds are a classic flavor combination, but feel free to swap in another kind of citrus zest in place of the lemon zest. Try orange, tangerine, lime, or even grapefruit zest.

| FAST PREP

cinnamon-pecan cake

PREP: 20 minutes | **SLOW COOK:** 2¼ to 2¾ hours (low) | **MAKES:** 12 servings

Nonstick cooking spray
1 egg, lightly beaten
1 8-oz. carton sour cream
½ cup milk
3 Tbsp. butter, melted
1 tsp. vanilla
1¾ cups all-purpose flour
½ cup sugar
1 tsp. baking soda
1 tsp. ground cinnamon
½ tsp. salt
½ cup chopped pecans, toasted (tip, *page 31*)
Caramel ice cream topping (optional)

1. Lightly coat a 3½- or 4-qt. slow cooker with cooking spray. In a large bowl whisk together the next five ingredients (through vanilla) until combined. Stir in flour, sugar, baking soda, cinnamon, and salt until smooth. Stir in pecans. Spoon batter into the prepared cooker.

2. Cover and cook on low 2¼ to 2¾ hours or until an instant-read thermometer inserted in cake registers between 190°F and 200°F and center appears nearly set, rotating crockery liner once halfway through cooking. Remove crockery liner from cooker. Cool on a wire rack 10 minutes. Loosen sides of cake and remove from cooker. Cool completely. If desired, drizzle with ice cream topping.

PER SERVING: *235 cal., 11 g fat (5 g sat. fat), 37 mg chol., 257 mg sodium, 30 g carb., 1 g fiber, 15 g sugars, 4 g pro.*

TOP IT OFF

You can get creative with the topping for this easy cake. Try chocolate syrup, butterscotch syrup, marshmallow topping, or sweetened whipped cream. Or serve each piece with a scoop of cinnamon or vanilla ice cream.

chocolate-marshmallow cake

PREP: 15 minutes | **SLOW COOK:** 2½ to 3½ hours (low) | **STAND:** 1 hour | **MAKES:** 12 servings

Nonstick cooking spray

3 eggs, lightly beaten

1 cup water

1 8-oz. carton sour cream

1 2-layer-size chocolate cake mix

1 cup all-purpose flour

1 cup sugar

1 cup tiny marshmallows

1 7-oz. jar marshmallow creme

¾ cup milk chocolate or semisweet chocolate pieces

6 graham cracker squares, broken into 1-inch pieces

1. Lightly coat the inside of a 6-qt. oval slow cooker with cooking spray. In a large bowl whisk together eggs, the water, and sour cream. Stir cake mix, flour, and sugar into egg mixture just until combined. Stir in marshmallows. Spoon batter into prepared cooker.

2. Cover and cook on low 2½ to 3½ hours or until an instant-read thermometer inserted in cake registers 180°F (center may still appear moist), rotating the crockery liner once halfway through cooking.

3. Drop spoonfuls of marshmallow creme over hot cake (it will spread as cake stands). Sprinkle with chocolate pieces. Remove crockery liner from cooker. Let stand, covered, 1 hour. Just before serving, top with graham cracker pieces.

PER SERVING: 479 cal., 13 g fat (7 g sat. fat), 61 mg chol., 351 mg sodium, 87 g carb., 2 g fiber, 54 g sugars, 7 g pro.

 | FAST PREP

apple-cherry cake

PREP: 20 minutes | **SLOW COOK:** 2¼ to 2¾ hours (low) | **MAKES:** 12 servings

Nonstick cooking spray

1 cup plain yogurt

½ cup milk

1 egg

3 Tbsp. butter, melted

1 tsp. vanilla

1¾ cups all-purpose flour

½ cup sugar

1 tsp. baking soda

1 tsp. apple pie spice

½ tsp. salt

1 cup chopped apple

½ cup chopped walnuts, toasted (tip, *page 31*)

½ cup dried tart red cherries

1. Lightly coat a 3½- or 4-qt. slow cooker with cooking spray; set aside. In a large bowl whisk together the next five ingredients (through vanilla) until combined. Stir in the next five ingredients (through salt) until smooth. Stir in remaining ingredients. Spoon batter into cooker.

2. Cover and cook on low 2¼ to 2¾ hours or until an instant-read thermometer inserted in cake registers between 190°F and 200°F and center appears nearly set, rotating crockery liner once halfway through cooking. Remove crockery liner from cooker. Cool on a wire rack 10 minutes. Loosen sides of cake and remove from cooker. Cool completely.

PER SERVING: *212 cal., 7 g fat (3 g sat. fat), 25 mg chol., 251 mg sodium, 33 g carb., 1 g fiber, 17 g sugars, 5 g pro.*

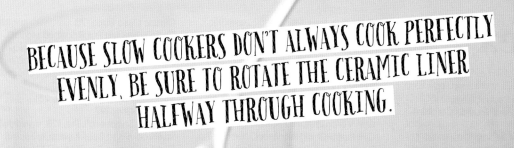

BECAUSE SLOW COOKERS DON'T ALWAYS COOK PERFECTLY EVENLY, BE SURE TO ROTATE THE CERAMIC LINER HALFWAY THROUGH COOKING.

metric information

PRODUCT DIFFERENCES

Most of the ingredients called for in the recipes in this book are available in most countries. However, some are known by different names. Here are some common American ingredients and their possible counterparts:

- Sugar (white) is granulated, fine granulated, or caster sugar.

- Powdered sugar is icing sugar.

- All-purpose flour is enriched bleached or unbleached white household flour. When self-rising flour is used in place of all-purpose flour in a recipe that calls for leavening, omit the leavening agent (baking soda or baking powder) and salt.

- Light-color corn syrup is golden syrup.

- Cornstarch is cornflour.

- Baking soda is bicarbonate of soda.

- Vanilla or vanilla extract is vanilla essence.

- Green, red, or yellow sweet peppers are capsicums or bell peppers.

- Golden raisins are sultanas.

VOLUME AND WEIGHT

The United States traditionally uses cup measures for liquid and solid ingredients. The chart (above right) shows the approximate imperial and metric equivalents. If you are accustomed to weighing solid ingredients, the following approximate equivalents will be helpful.

- 1 cup butter, caster sugar, or rice = 8 ounces = ½ pound = 250 grams

- 1 cup flour = 4 ounces = ¼ pound = 125 grams

- 1 cup icing sugar = 5 ounces = 150 grams

- Canadian and U.S. volume for a cup measure is 8 fluid ounces (237 ml), but the standard metric equivalent is 250 ml.

- 1 British imperial cup is 10 fluid ounces.

- In Australia, 1 tablespoon equals 20 ml, and there are 4 teaspoons in the Australian tablespoon.

- Spoon measures are used for small amounts of ingredients. Although the size of the tablespoon varies slightly in different countries, for practical purposes and for recipes in this book, a straight substitution is all that's necessary. Measurements made using cups or spoons always should be level unless stated otherwise.

COMMON WEIGHT RANGE REPLACEMENTS

Imperial / U.S.	Metric
½ ounce	15 g
1 ounce	25 g or 30 g
4 ounces (¼ pound)	115 g or 125 g
8 ounces (½ pound)	225 g or 250 g
16 ounces (1 pound)	450 g or 500 g
1¼ pounds	625 g
1½ pounds	750 g
2 pounds or 2¼ pounds	1,000 g or 1 Kg

OVEN TEMPERATURE EQUIVALENTS

Fahrenheit Setting	Celsius Setting	Gas Setting
300°F	150°C	Gas Mark 2 (very low)
325°F	160°C	Gas Mark 3 (low)
350°F	180°C	Gas Mark 4 (moderate)
375°F	190°C	Gas Mark 5 (moderate)
400°F	200°C	Gas Mark 6 (hot)
425°F	220°C	Gas Mark 7 (hot)
450°F	230°C	Gas Mark 8 (very hot)
475°F	240°C	Gas Mark 9 (very hot)
500°F	260°C	Gas Mark 10 (extremely hot)
Broil	Broil	Grill

*Electric and gas ovens may be calibrated using Celsius. However, for an electric oven, increase Celsius setting 10 to 20 degrees when cooking above 160°C. For convection or forced air ovens (gas or electric), lower the temperature setting 25°F/10°C when cooking at all heat levels.

BAKING PAN SIZES

Imperial / U.S.	Metric
9×1½-inch round cake pan	22- or 23×4-cm (1.5 L)
9×1½-inch pie plate	22- or 23×4-cm (1 L)
8×8×2-inch square cake pan	20×5-cm (2 L)
9×9×2-inch square cake pan	22- or 23×4.5-cm (2.5 L)
11×7×1½-inch baking pan	28×17×4-cm (2 L)
2-quart rectangular baking pan	30×19×4.5-cm (3 L)
13×9×2-inch baking pan	34×22×4.5-cm (3.5 L)
15×10×1-inch jelly roll pan	40×25×2-cm
9×5×3-inch loaf pan	23×13×8-cm (2 L)
2-quart casserole	2 L

U.S. / STANDARD METRIC EQUIVALENTS

⅛ teaspoon = 0.5 ml	
¼ teaspoon = 1 ml	
½ teaspoon = 2 ml	
1 teaspoon = 5 ml	
1 tablespoon = 15 ml	
2 tablespoons = 25 ml	
¼ cup = 2 fluid ounces = 50 ml	
⅓ cup = 3 fluid ounces = 75 ml	
½ cup = 4 fluid ounces = 125 ml	
⅔ cup = 5 fluid ounces = 150 ml	
¾ cup = 6 fluid ounces = 175 ml	
1 cup = 8 fluid ounces = 250 ml	
2 cups = 1 pint = 500 ml	
1 quart = 1 litre	